BILL JONES'
Notes from the
TURNING SHOP

BILL JONES'
Notes from the
TURNING SHOP

Guild of Master Craftsman Publications Ltd

This collection first published in this form 1996 by
Guild of Master Craftsman Publications Ltd,
166 High Street, Lewes,
East Sussex BN7 lXU

ISBN 1 86108 017 4

Designed by Teresa Dearlove

Typefaces: Cheltenham and Simoncini Garamond

Colour separation by Viscan Graphics, Singapore
Printed in Hong Kong by H & Y Printing Ltd.

Safety Note

The working methods contained in this book have been developed and perfected by Bill Jones, a highly skilled, professional turner, over many years. Descriptions of particular skills and general working practices are for historical interest – they are not instructional. Readers should be aware of safe working methods, and exercise common sense and caution in the workshop. Please refer to 'Health and Safety' on pages 136 and 137 – your safety is your responsibility.

ENCOURAGEMENT.

Ho! there, turner, Up man!
And wend you swiftly lathewards while you may
There to turn the hours away
With deft & cunning strokes of keen-edged tool
A rapier-point whose foes are manifold,
Some thrusting forth strong shields of stubborn opposition,
Some meeting blade with undisguised delight
As though a premonition of their final shape
Inspired them with impatient zest to be transformed.
For live materials oft are sentient things
Their very forms & textures are their own true voice
Imparting knowledge to the keen, receptive ear
Of craftsmen with perception thats inborn.
Who dare scorn the product of that esoteric bond?
Who crows, asmirk at honest bent
Of one who is at least sincere,
Seeking nothing but the rare delight
Of fashioning a trinket to his own design.
Not the turner, for he alone
Has trod the tortuous uphill path
From fumbling to perfection.
He knows too well that things which are to him
Symetrical & true in all detail,
To others strike an inharmonious chord,
And therefore holds his peace.
Strive on then turner
And make your tools obey your will
Be of good heart, for to the empathetic eye
The unpretentious trifle YOU consider good,
However over-shadowed by a more ambitious thing
Will not on that account be rendered bad.

11

Contents

Introduction

My earliest recollections are of running pulleys connected by string to a shafting, which powered half a dozen lathes in my father's shop. It never occurred to me that I was going to be anything but a turner, and I always felt inordinately blessed to have a father who was unique. Nobody else at all had an ivory turner for a father! While shops like ours were becoming obsolete, and people were subject to more and more 'progress' and modernization, I was the fixed point in a changing age – an age where craftsmanship, work satisfaction and even employment itself were to be things of the past.

Now, whilst the trade of hardwood and ivory turner has more or less disappeared, there are still plenty of woodturners plying their craft. Many of them are fully satisfied with all they do, and are contented. But there are some who would love to expand their present capabilities and the range of their work. It is for the benefit of these turners, as well as those who simply enjoy reading about how it used to be done, that I am writing these details of the old trade.

The basics of hand turning can be taught by any competent teacher, but the student's progress is entirely up to the individual. It is far from easy to make tools comply with one's exact requirements, but sooner or later they will, and when they are fully under control, there need be no limit to one's turning aspirations.

In all branches of turnery you will find good, bad and indifferent examples of work – this is entirely due to the turners and not the genre. I have found (sometimes in the most unlikely places) such marvellous pieces of work that really encourage me. I have also learned my limitations so that work I marvel at, but that I know is beyond my capabilities, I can enjoy without getting frustrated. Craftsmanship is an individual thing, and no-one can excel at everything.

The main asset a turner can have is optimism, and the longer one continues, the higher may one's sights be set. Then there will be no trophy more alluring than your next masterpiece. It's all up to you, but meanwhile remember that G. K. Chesterton said, 'If a thing is worth doing, it's worth doing badly!' And there is no such thing as a turner who didn't begin with bad work.

For me, masterpieces are for red-letter days. I'm content to be simply turning, even simple, repetitous jobs. When tooling is easy, turning is always enjoyable. It is for me, because I can still see the wheels going round. I can control every movement of those wheels, so I have the perfect lathe, a machine sought in vain by the vast majority of turners. That is why I'm more at home in the turning shop than anywhere else, regardless what work is on the stocks. I hope you enjoy your visit. I am certain you won't be bored!

Chapter 1 ● *Variable-Speed* DEVICES

*B*efore the days of man-made materials and plastics, everything used to be made of natural materials like wood, bone, ivory, horn, shell, etc. There were always woodturners of course, but many of the other materials were handled by 'hardwood and ivory turners', sometimes known as 'bone grubbers'. They used different tools from the woodturner, tools that the woodturner would call 'scrapers', just a whit disparagingly, but which, used on their harder materials, were really turning tools *par excellence*!

The hardwood and ivory turner's *coup de maitre*, however, was his ability to cut threads with the screw tool or hand chaser. This enabled him to accomplish every sort of joined and screwed work in bone, horn, ivory, and the dense hardwoods, and also to make his own boxwood, lignum or hornbeam lathe chucks, which screwed onto the mandrel.

SLOW-SPEED LATHES

Of course, a *sine qua non* of thread cutting is a very slow lathe speed. In the days of the treadle lathe this was no problem as the speed

Prizewinning chesspieces, 1961

was foot controlled, but with power-driven lathes, a means of slowing the speed had to be devised. Professional turners always found a working method, but one thing they never had was lathes that had to be turned off to stop them! To this old hardwood and ivory turner, this is the enigma of the twentieth century.

Left *Shafting pulley for the Acorn lathe, 10in (250mm)*

FOOT-CONTROLLED LATHES

Usually, lathes had fast and loose pulleys: one moved the flat leather belt over to the left hand (loose) pulley, and, as the mandrel slowed down before stopping, the thread was cut with the chaser – the speed of the mandrel was adjusted manually, by adroitly shifting the belt. Sometimes the lathe had a luxurious mechanical device enabling the turner to shift the belt over to the loose pulley, but craftily leaving it partially on the fast one. (This was not the idea of the manufacturer of course, but devised by the wit of the turner, who always has to improvise!) The result of this was to give a nice slow speed which gradually got faster.

When I started work again after WWII, I was turning in a shaving brush factory for a short time, and I worked on a large, hollow mandrel lathe, turning two- and three-piece handles by hand. The lathe drive was by flat belt from an overhead shafting, giving a mandrel speed of about 2,300rpm – miles too fast for screw cutting. However, as the sketch below shows, the belt could be positioned by a fork, and adjusted by a thumb screw at any position across the fast and loose pulleys. It was a reflex action to whip the belt over to the loose pulley and then fix it with the screw about ¼in (6mm) onto the fast pulley. As the lathe progressively

Hollow mandrel lathe with thumb-screw belt adjuster

picked up speed, you slowed it down again with a hand on the chuck as a brake.

The adjustment of speed without stopping the motor had another advantage – it helped to reduce tool chatter and made precision hand turning of hard materials much easier, as with the popular two-piece saucer pattern shown below. For this we used tubular erinoid or catalin, cutting the inside thread of the top section first and then cutting it off. We then cut the male thread on the bottom, screwing the top onto it and turning the complete shape.

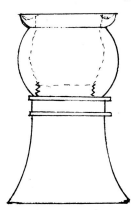

Saucer pattern, two-piece shaving brush handle

Here's something I read which might interest you: 'Douglas Bomford (an engineer working in the 1930s), like many other inventive engineers, before and since, became inflicted by the desire to make an infinitely variable speed gear. Like the alchemist's dream of turning base metal into gold, the pursuit of this ideal form of transmission, like the perpetual motion machine, can become an obsession.'

FOOT-CONTROLLED SPEED

As many of my friends know, I've always used foot-controlled variable speed and have found it quite perfect for my requirements – and absolutely indispensable. Bertram (my father), who used it extensively, said it was an old Birmingham idea, but exactly who invented it and when I've no idea.

In Bertram's turning shop, in the 1920s, he had a shafting driven by a 3hp motor underneath the long timber bench; it served four lathes. Each lathe had a hinged back carriage behind it which was driven by a 1in (25mm) flat leather belt, from a 10in (254mm) wooden pulley on the shafting. The back carriage rises and tightens the belt as the foot pedal is depressed. On lifting the foot, the back carriage goes down and the belt slips, giving reduced speed, or even stopping the lathe.

This foot movement becomes as natural as using a car accelerator so that, when working, the control you have over the lathe greatly simplifies the process of superb turning and increases the turner's confidence beyond measure. Also, as the lathe was used for most other operations, such as using the circular saw, grinding wheel, sanding disc, polishing buff, carving cutters, etc., the fact that your foot automatically comes off the pedal to stop the lathe at once, is a very reassuring factor.

SIMPLE TO CONSTRUCT

The basic idea is simple to construct, and no precision work is required – I have never yet encountered a turning job where a precise speed was necessary. As long as the maximum speed is about right, my foot can do the rest; I can come right down to 100rpm or less for jobs such as cutting a thread up to the shoulder on a necklace fastener, about $\frac{1}{16}$in (2mm) long. Wonderful!

THE BEAUTY of the contrivance is its infinite potential for adjustment

As you will see from the sketches right, you need a length of 1½in (38mm) angle iron, cut in the right places and bent cold: measurements are not critical, but not less than 12 x 5in (300 x 120mm). The pulleys are turned from beech or whatever, a flat 4–4¾in (100–120mm) for the motor (unless you can find a cast iron one) and the same for the back carriage so that it runs at the same speed as the motor – usually 1,440rpm. Joined to the flat back carriage pulley is the vee pulley which drives the lathe. To calculate the size of the vee driver, divide the lathe speed you require (about 2,400rpm does me) by the back carriage speed and multiply the result by the diameter of the mandrel pulley. I have back carriage speed as 1,400rpm, lathe speed required as 2,400rpm, and diameter of mandrel pulley as 3in (75mm), ergo: 2,400/1,400 x 3/1 = 5in (2,400/1,400 x 75/1 = 125mm).

It may suit some turners to have a range of maximum speeds commensurate with the stepped mandrel pulley: in that case you must

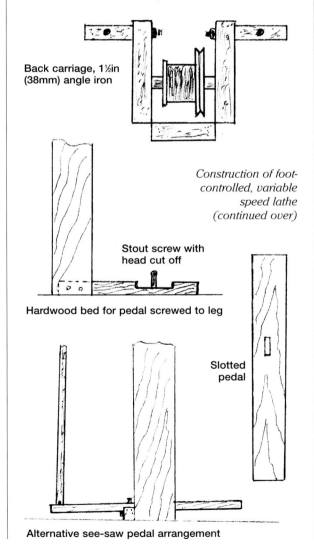

Back carriage, 1½in (38mm) angle iron

Construction of foot-controlled, variable speed lathe (continued over)

Stout screw with head cut off

Hardwood bed for pedal screwed to leg

Slotted pedal

Alternative see-saw pedal arrangement

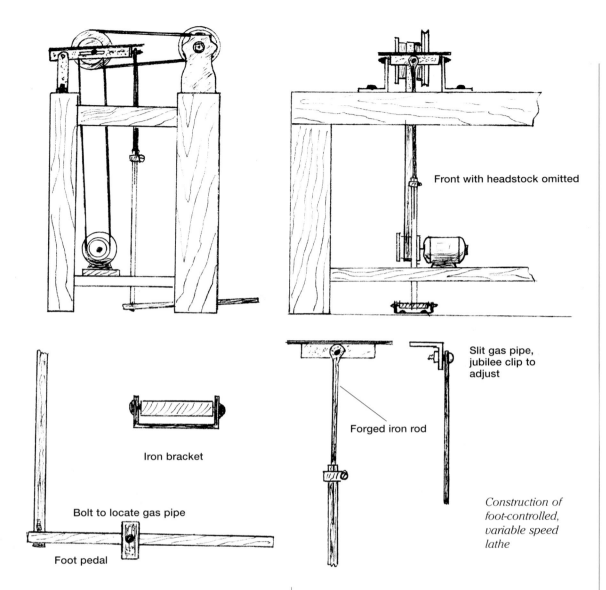

Front with headstock omitted

Iron bracket

Bolt to locate gas pipe

Foot pedal

Slit gas pipe,
jubilee clip to
adjust

Forged iron rod

*Construction of
foot-controlled,
variable speed
lathe*

exactly duplicate the same pulley on the back carriage. I make a boxwood shaft and recess the pulleys to take ball-races each side – a couple of old ones of about 2in (50mm) diameter. A couple of small coach screws will secure the shaft within the angle iron frame which is slotted both sides for adjustment to the lathe belt tension.

The 1in (25mm) flat leather belting from motor to back carriage is cut to length so that when the pedal is hard down, the front top bar of the back carriage is exactly midway between the lathe driving belt. This keeps the lathe belt at the right tension, and you get a positive drive. When the flat belt stretches –

which is rare because it gives almost no trouble and lasts for ever! – you simply shorten it until, again, the front of the back carriage is midway when at maximum speed. The rod twixt pedal and back carriage is simple to adjust and the beauty of the contrivance is its infinite potential for adjustment and the almost complete lack of cost, not to mention the tremendous personal satisfaction in accomplishing so valuable a panacea.

And what have you got? Well, you know how a talking robot sounds? That is your lathe at present. Now hear a real human orator giving to his voice all the pitch, pace and power that holds an audience spellbound: that's the difference!

GUARANTEE

With foot-controlled variable speed, you can make your lathe talk! When you are learning, when the tools won't go right for you, when you get chattering and ribbed work, variable speed won't make you into a marvellous turner instantly, but I guarantee it'll make your turning much easier, far more enjoyable, and attended with far less frustration and impatience. You don't have to stop the motor, and you can run the belt backwards manually when using a tap. Wow!

I run four lathes with this apparatus and two others by sewing machine clutch motors, which are very good too. If you are looking for one, make sure that it's not less than ¼ horse power, and that it has a speed around 1,400rpm, as some are double speed.

I know that many lathes are totally enclosed, but nobody has made an inviolable rule that a

Prizewinning chesspieces, 1987

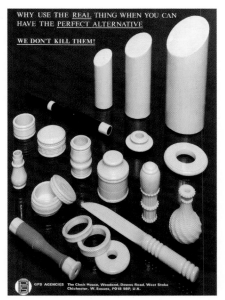

WHY USE THE REAL THING WHEN YOU CAN HAVE THE PERFECT ALTERNATIVE

WE DON'T KILL THEM!

GPS AGENCIES The Clock House, Woodend, Downs Road, West Stoke
Chichester, W. Sussex, PO18 9BP, U.K.

Alternative ivory pieces

turner only has one lathe! The old hardwood and ivory turners never knew the luxury of buying new lathes! They picked up second-hand headstocks and often non-matching tailstocks which they raised up with slivers of wood when required. Why, when I started my first turning shop . . . But that's another story.

Chapter 2 ● *Repetitive* PRACTICE

Some time ago, at an auction sale held by the Society of Ornamental Turners, a small book was knocked down to me for a tenner or so. Its title? *Turning for Beginners* (being elementary instruction in the art of turning in wood and metal etc.), by James Lukin, dated 1906. It is described in a famous turning bibliography as 'a very elementary trifle'. A roar of laughter arose from the ranks of my friends (flatterers!), but I didn't mind! I have a number of Lukin's books, which make delightful reading, and when one loves the art and craft of turning as much as I do, elementary trifles are often more enjoyable than engrossing conglomerations of technical jargon that leave me as wise at the end as I was at the start – usually, I never reach the end.

I do not blame myself for failing to understand obscure writings. It simply means that an otherwise brilliant mind lacks the essential ability to make its meaning clear to the ordinary reader. And if they're not kind enough even to try, then I don't bother anyway. My gratitude goes to the able ones who do take the trouble to make their message clear and understandable.

I was practically born in the turning shop and I don't think I ever wanted to be anywhere else beyond the normal Walter Mitty fantasies everyone probably has. I wouldn't know if there are any gifted turners. Most of these so-called gifts accrue to those who work hard at their chosen activity while others are out enjoying themselves, and then rush up with their infuriating '. . .phew! I wish I had your gift' swindle. You've met 'em!

SO-CALLED gifts accrue to those who work hard

When I started I was a rotten turner (who isn't!), and it was years before I admitted to myself that maybe I wasn't too bad. Then the pendulum swung the other way, and I felt superior to most other turners, for there were practically none left in my trade of hardwood and ivory turners. And then I got a shock! I met the ornamental turners and never recovered!

No, they couldn't compete with my kind of work, and weren't interested anyway, but they could achieve a perfection, a higher standard, than all the work I had been used to. From that time on my purpose changed. I always turned out good work of merchantable quality, but

Left *Polishing on the buff*

9

now I strove to achieve a better article, even if it cut my profits quite a lot. I ceased to be a mere tradesman, and work became something beyond a means of livelihood.

A chap who prefers Monday morning to Sunday has got to be envied! I'd always been taught by Bertram that the 'bloke who says he can't do a thing is usually right' , so when I struck a snag I didn't say 'I can't do that', I said, 'I can't do that this way', and I found an easier method if possible. Only gradually does real skill come, and I can take no credit because I've had to stick at it to earn a living – and at many things I'm still a beginner.

That is why it's a great shame that a youth has to wait until he has a family to support before he leaves school and starts work! A 'prentice turner is double-useless for many weeks and just isn't worth much in the way of wages. An older man cannot work for nothing, so all he can do is to equip himself with a lathe and practise at home.

The snag is that the impetus to keep him working on the lathe until he does become proficient is not always there. As a kid you've got to stick with it, maybe with the guvnor standing behind you, telling you what a B. fool you are, but, in the privacy of one's garage, it takes real determination to stick at a job you are making a muck-up of until it does come right. Yet that is what must be done. Further, you want to enjoy it and not regard it as a penance – remember, you will make progress despite all setbacks. Failure is one of the basic freedoms, and is but a detour on the road to success.

REPETITION WORK

Some of my turning friends were discussing work they'd done; one said, 'I had to make several of them. I was bored stiff!'. Oh dear, oh dear! Poor fellah! He was actually a rare good turner as it happens, but if he couldn't enjoy a little repetitive work, he is missing something!

Some turners scorn repetition work, and it's true that your experienced turner can turn almost anything to order first time, but he has to take as much time as he needs, and he feels his way like a musician playing something new: obviously he's going to play it miles better the twenty-third time.

When a number of items have to be turned, like chess pieces for example, the work improves, the time it takes is cut considerably, and the tooling becomes easier and attended with greater satisfaction – the more you do, the easier they become. So, always welcome repetition work as it increases skill. When someone picks up your pawn, you won't be wondering if he'll notice the striae or other defects because you enjoyed making it and it was easy. Turning is like singing – if it's easy it's sheer heaven, but if it's forced – ugh! Am I getting through to you?

Sir Malcolm Sargent (known as Flash Harry!) was asked how he could possibly enjoy conducting popular pieces hundreds of times. 'Easy', he replied, 'I always listen with the ears of one hearing it for the first time.' He liked repetition work.

I spent my first five years on repetition work, turning and cutting screws in bone and erinoid (a rather pleasant casein material from which all the fountain pens and knitting needles used to be made). At the end I thought I was unskilled compared with Bertram, who did all the best work and carving. It was only after WWII, when I was slung in the deep end, on my own in my first workshop, that I learned, to my surprise, that my five years had given me jolly nearly all the skills I needed.

CATHETER PLUGS

When I began in my new shop, my main work for a while was turning tapered catheter plugs at the rate of 10 gross a week. Catheter plugs were used in hospitals (briefly) and thrown

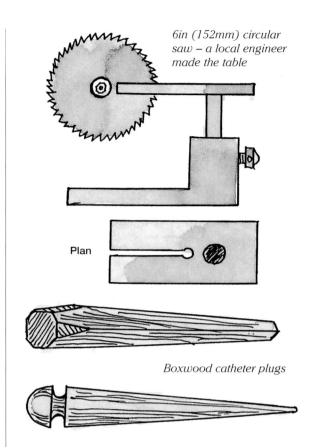

6in (152mm) circular saw – a local engineer made the table

Plan

Boxwood catheter plugs

away. They were cut from the boxwood offcuts of the ruler makers. A 6in (152mm) circular saw running on the lathe produced 10 gross of cut pieces in 1½ days.

The pieces were banged into an iron chuck with a 1½lb (680g) ball pein hammer, the handle of which was cut down to 5in (127mm). The taper was quickly turned shining smooth with a ⅜in (10mm) gouge and a 1in (25mm) chisel, at the rate of three a minute. They were then reversed and tapped into a boxwood chuck with a tapered hole to fit the plugs. The knob end was finished even quicker with a ¼in (6mm) gouge and a narrow, round nose tool made from a three square file.

I made a boxwood hammer, like the one shown below, to tap them out with. The iron chucks, of which the lathes had sets with varying holes, were well scarred with years of clouting because it was usual to bang everything into a chuck. They were stopped with a plug of bone, horn or iron, as appropriate, and hollowed, slightly tapered, to take the catheter plugs.

MAGIC CARPET

Those who turn purely for pleasure will wonder seriously how anyone could work at jobs like those for any length of time and still like lathes! I suppose the reason is that if the lathe runs well, the tools are sharp and well under control, and you have a day before you to produce first class, clean turnery, the very fact that your own two hands – which have become precision tools through years of practice – are doing something useful, enables you to let them enjoy the pleasure of making things while you can take a magic carpet ride in imagination, where e'er you will. All I know is, there is something soothing and delightful to me in simply turning.

I had a turning aspirant in my shop some time ago, and being a devotee of numerous arts and crafts, of course his eyes began to gleam and sparkle as he watched me turning some lemonwood organ draw-stop knobs. After a couple of visits (he couldn't stay away!) he intimated that a turner's life, one like mine

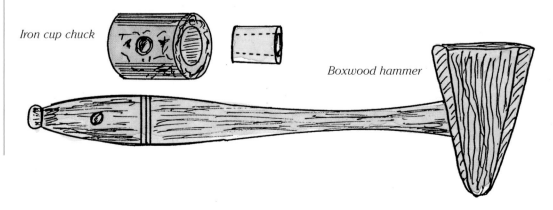

Iron cup chuck

Boxwood hammer

at least, must be a happy one, and he wondered if there might be a chance . . . ? I told him that I could fix him up with some work to try which, while not causing me any inconvenience, would certainly establish whether or not he'd be suited to the job.

And so, a couple of days later, he came along to try turning braille erasers in casein rod on the hollow mandrel lathe, with a small, self-centring chuck. My braille erasers go all over the world and the only important part is the business end – the tip – which is ⅛in (3mm) in diameter, and must be perfectly flat and smooth.

It should, of course, be well-shaped and finished, but little is critical, so a beginner can enjoy the work with the minimum of damage. Actually, when I am making a batch of these I can forget them. Because my mind is so busy I'd keep stopping to investigate some red herring which called for attention, but for one thing – I keep a record player going with LPs of Scottish dance bands or some Vivaldi or the like, and that keeps the rhythm going lickety split. I find this even more enjoyable than some abstruse turning problem.

Braille eraser

Well, I set him to work on some simple shapes on spare lengths of casein rod, using a round tool, square tool, point tool and screever, to get him used to things gradually. He began very carefully, after several demonstrations, and did nothing disastrous. I thought, in fact he's a darned sight better than I was when I started, but then, he was 40 and could use his hands. In half an hour he was turning shapes something like that shown above reasonably, along with all sorts of other shapeless attempts which result from trying to make sense with unfamiliar tools. But

although he had two sessions of about four hours, on two separate days, he just never turned one decent eraser. Some were near, but not one was acceptable.

He won't try again because he has the idea that if one has the aptitude for a certain skill, it will quickly be revealed, and if it is not, it is less traumatic to chuck it. 'I'm too old', he said.

He realized that simple hand tools were not just placed on the tee rest and gently pushed into the work. Each cutting edge has to be carefully applied at the precise angle, both laterally and obliquely, and the handle moved up and down, and left to right or right to left, and the lathe speed has to be regulated by the foot pedal (variable speed – not treadle) to the requisite rpm, to obtain a good result without chatter marks.

As I told him, you have all these things to get right and, at first, it is impossible to think of everything at once. He was so occupied in his correct tooling at one stage that he forgot to keep the lathe in motion at all. Oft, he would apply the tool upside down.

REFLEX ACTION

The only way for all these things to come together with success, is for it to become a reflex action. One can't play a piano without loads of practice. Think of all your fingers playing all the different keys in the right sequence and at the correct volume so perfectly that the incredible human brain is able to detect if just one of those fingers hits a wrong note! Thinking of that – well! – who the dickens couldn't turn a silly braille eraser?!! Yet even this has to be learnt, and in only one way – stick at it until it does become possible and easy. You have to want to do it enough.

Back in the 1920s, Bertram employed a young man who could not turn; I mean he was worse than anybody had a right to be, yet he genuinely liked turning, although Bertram said several times, 'You'll have to go Harry, you're never going to get the hang of it!'. Still he begged for another week or so, and against all odds he did become a good turner. Well, I mean, you try hammering a 2in (50mm) length of ⅜in (10mm) bone into an iron chuck, and chasing a perfect thread on it. As soon as you touch it with the gouge it flies out! I used to sit on his bench by the hour, watching him while he told me stories he made up . . . Turning is no gift, it is simply perseverance.

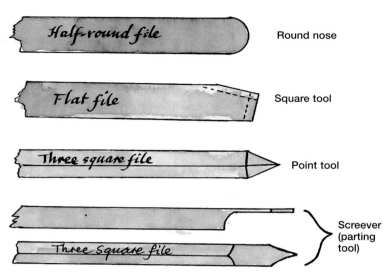

Many files make useful turning tools

TOOLS

I use quite a few files for my turning tools. I find them as efficacious, and often more convenient than the manufactured carbon steel and high-speed steel (HSS) ones which I also use, but please, choose which you prefer and whatever is convenient. I have learned that tools and grinding angles are not fixed and immutable like the laws of the Medes and the Persians! Each turner gleans his own experience and it is his finished work that reveals his skill, not his tools. I took some of my tools to a turners' meeting once and one old cough drop remarked that, on appearance, he wouldn't pick 'em up in the street! Of course, I have some better looking ones too.

Erinoid handle

Take my square tool in HSS, above right. Its angle is no different from that of the skew, yet it would be described as a scraper. It is not. Tilted and applied in the proper manner, it cuts just like a skew, but can turn bone and other hard materials: 'scraper' is an unknown term to the hardwood and ivory turner. The screever, above right, is a parting tool used for stock up to about 2in (50mm) in diameter. The

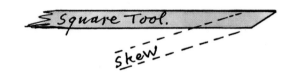

smaller ones are okay in short handles, but for larger cuts, the overall length of tool and handle is about 12in (305mm). The point of the screever is ground, not stoned.

Parting requires skill, and the tools used seldom wear out – they break. You start by entering, making a slight margin for clearance. Now here's where the longer handle comes in. You do not use your hands for applying pressure, only guidance. The screever is driven in by your body weight, guiding from the solar plexus, and you'll be surprised at the control you have. By gently easing the tool in, and very slightly tilting left and right, you'll provide a clearance which obviates binding. If some binding does occur, scrape off the burnt stuff and apply a candle.

My turning won't suit everyone – of course it won't – but I hope you may find something of value in these notes, even if it's only my point tool, above, which is ground to a three-sided pyramid, turns perfect beads and performs a variety of different functions, yet is almost unknown.

Chapter 3 ● *Cutting* SCREW THREADS

*L*ike most manipulative skills, screw cutting by hand chaser has been described in a number of different ways, and doubtless those describers are able (I hope) to cut perfectly good threads, even though their methods differ from mine. Like the sergeant, I can say, 'You can do it the easy way or the hard way. And the easy way ain't easy. And the hard way's ruddy hard!'

I think my easy way works, and I hope anyone who tries doesn't give up quickly because, if you persevere, you will certainly succeed. I can't promise you'll cut good threads every time, because no-one does. There is always the odd failure that teaches one that mistakes can happen. If I'm cutting a thread in front of an audience, I do what Mozart did on one occasion, when he played

14

Above Cutting thread on a king's stem

violin in a concerto: he warned his audience that he wasn't very good with the fiddle, played like an angel and brought the house down!

WORK attended with risk has to be respected

I made a disgraceful muck-up cutting a screw the other day, when showing a young lad. I began, with careless bravado, to perform a simple job, and some quirkish gremlin said, 'We will take you down a peg my lad, and show you that work attended with risk has to be respected, and mistakes are always possible, however unlikely they seem.' (I covered it up all right though!) After he'd gone, of course, I couldn't put a foot – or a chaser – wrong!

FOUR FACTORS
At least four factors must be considered in screw cutting:

1 lathe speed;
2 position of tee rest;
3 the tool itself – condition, length of handle, etc.;
4 method of striking thread.

All these things can be arranged and manipulated differently with equal success, the only inviolable rule being that, regardless of the lathe speed, for every complete revolution the screw tool, commonly known as a chaser, needs to be traversed to the left, a distance equal to the interval between two of its teeth. It must be admitted that this information is of no value whatever, because hand chasing depends for its success not upon theories, but on 'getting the knack of the thing'.

An engineer sets up a train of gears to ensure that the lathe speed and tool traverse are precisely co-ordinated to cut whatever screw he desires. To perform the same thing freehand would seen quite impossible, yet the hand and the eye are the finest and most adaptable 'tools' in the world, and what it takes a train of gears to accomplish, these superior tools can do very well when they get the feel of it.

Of course, everything depends on how much you want to cut threads. If you aren't prepared to spend as much effort (though far less money) as a golfer does to reduce his handicap, you must put up with push-fit boxes, which I always leave out of my personal repertoire, as I feel they will loosen or tighten sooner or later. If too tight, you carefully try to separate the lid when lo!, your two hands suddenly fly apart and all your gramophone needles or what-have-you fly in all directions and stick in your feet when you're going to bed!

Two tools are needed for thread cutting: an outside, and an inside chaser. Chasers, when new, need a little preparation. They must slide freely over the tee rest or armrest, so the rubbing surfaces must have their sharp corners and any rough places removed on the emery wheel and oilstone. Sharpening is done on the top face, which I hollow grind and rub on the oilstone. If the first, or leading tooth is dull (you can observe this clearly if you look closely), the chaser will perform badly because that is the tooth that does the work; the rest just follow. The top of the tee must be perfectly smooth and rubbed with oilstone. Additionally, a rub with a candle helps free movement enormously, not

Inside and outside hand chasers

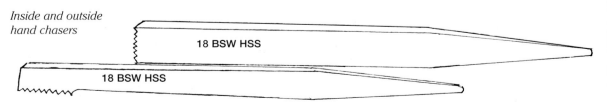

18 BSW HSS

18 BSW HSS

15

only for chasers, but for all other tools as well. Watch the frequency that a snooker player chalks his cue – that's how often you need to rub a candle over your tee rest.

Chasers should be fitted into comfortable handles not less than 5in (125mm) long. The overall length of the tool in its handle should be between 9–12in (230–300mm), the longer handles being necessary for coarse threads. Chasers range in size from 3–40 teeth per inch (25mm), but anything below 8 was so rarely called for, it was usual to soften an old flat file, and file the teeth ourselves.

For the purpose of practice, any odd pieces of material can be used, such as dense hardwoods and plastics like casein, polyester resin etc.: anything between ½–2in (10–50mm) will be suitable. Fix your piece in the lathe, turn it cylindrical and face – you may round the front edge if you prefer. A medium chaser, 20–24 teeth per inch, will be the easiest.

Fix the tee parallel with, and about ¾in (20mm) away from the work, a little below centre height. Hold the chaser at the end of the handle, with the right forefinger running along it, and place the tool upon the tee. Now, whereas your woodturner will normally have most of his left hand above the tool, the hardwood and ivory turners do not. In their case, the fingers of the left hand are all below the tee, with the thumb on top or at the left side of the tool. Further, whereas in normal woodturning the cutting tool is brought above and then downwards into the cut, here the tool is brought from below into a dragging cut which would be scraping softwood, but of course, turns the harder materials.

FULCRUM

So, the fingers of the left hand are below the tee – maybe around the pedestal if convenient – and the left thumb is on top of the chaser where it lies on the tee. This is the fulcrum or swivelling point and it must be appreciated that

anything which restricts the free movement of the chaser spells ruin! That is why we have a goodly space between the tee and the work, and why the tool handle is held at the end – indeed, if the right forefinger proves restrictive, let it join the others around the handle as I often do. It feels not quite right, but it works.

Now! With the chaser just out of contact with the work and the left thumb holding the tool down on the tee, describe a series of clockwise circles, with the tool handle held close to your solar plexus. This is the striking movement which must be practised, in a relaxed manner, until it feels natural. Set the lathe in gentle motion – about 150–500rpm – and, after a few preliminary circles just out of range, strike the thread with the lightest of touches when the tool is moving to the left at the bottom of its circular movement.

Use the middle of the chaser to strike on the rounded corner of the work. The second and following strokes become easier as the thread takes the tool along. Use short strokes with light pressure to deepen the thread as it carries the chaser a little further on at each stroke. By applying the tool lightly and below centre height, there is no difficulty in dropping the points exactly in the grooves already cut. The senses of touch and timing are vastly important and progress should be inevitable after a little practice.

DRUNK

Theoretically, it would appear impossible to contrive the necessary relationship twixt lathe speed and tool traverse to obtain a true thread by hand and eye alone, yet in practice, the hand becomes accustomed to the feel of a true thread so that, should the chaser have been moved a trifle too fast or slow, the noticeable kink or bend will be felt. This is known as a drunk thread which, if slight, can often be corrected by the adept, with further chasing. If not, the screw can be turned down with a flat

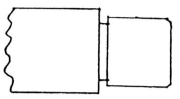

A shallow groove helps prevent thread damage

tool for further attempts.

To reduce the thread diameter to a specific size, the screw should always be turned down with a flat tool to remove the tops of the threads, but leaving enough to guide the chaser in finishing to size.

When a screw needs to be cut up to a shoulder, it is necessary to face the surface of the shoulder and turn a shallow groove, as can be seen above. This prevents the chaser being carried into the shoulder and, by a sudden jar, damaging the thread. The manipulation of the chaser, when working up to the shoulder, requires extra lightness and care. A very slow lathe speed makes it easier to remove the tool at the precise moment. This is where the foot-controlled variable speed device is invaluable.

remove the slightly flattened crest diameter, as this makes the crest less likely to crumble. Finally, the screw is reduced to its correct length, and rounded slightly at the end.

ARMREST

An armrest is necessary for cutting internal threads. Although not obtainable in shops, they are easily made – use a 7in (175mm) mild steel crook in a 12in (300mm) handle. No hardening is required, but it is essential to ensure that it is well stoned, for friction-free sliding over the tee.

No hard and fast measurements are involved; a giant would obviously make a much larger armrest than a midget. The crook end is merely to prevent the turning tool sliding off, so simply bending up about ¼in (6mm) is ample.

This tool is indispensable to the hardwood turner as, tucked under the left armpit with the

Armrest — Inside tool — Half round file

You may find that tilting the chaser very slightly to the left helps in producing clean threads. The more you use hand turning tools, the more you will learn how they behave when moved and tilted in various ways. These movements, which you get to know by experience and experiment, become automatic in time. You also learn how different materials 'prefer to be cut', as Frank Pain so rightly used to say. We never stop learning something new, although we forget some old things of course!

For finishing the screw, especially on wood, a flat tool is used – infinitesimally – to bring the tops of the threads level, and the chaser is re-applied lightly, but not enough to entirely

crook resting on the tee, it forms an additional tool rest for working at the face without having to adjust the tee 'thwartships', or at right angles to the lathe axis, where it is not half so pleasurable or convenient as the armrest. Try it for turning spheres or ovals, or some accurate drilling – don't just think about it lazily!

The aperture to be threaded is hollowed cylindrically and slightly rounded at the front. It is also recessed at the bottom of the hole (if you happen to have the luxury of a suitable tool handy), to allow time for the chaser to be withdrawn before it jars at the bottom.

I must tell you that hardwood and ivory turners never bought tools they could make – if they did, somebody would knock a

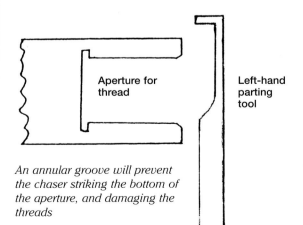

Inside tool – half round file

ha'penny off their prices, and they'd lose work – but anybody who wishes, please, buy all the tools you want. Just grind the teeth off the face where the cutting edge is, and off the back where it rubs the tool rest. Grind it to about 45° (angle is not at all precise) and rub it on an India stone, and you have a lovely inside tool. You can even call it a scraper if you wish, although, as I've said before, hardwood and ivory turners don't scrape, they turn.

Open the hole with an inside tool, using the armrest – here's how. Tuck the handle under the left armpit. Lean with the right hip against the bench, facing the work, and project the armrest, hook uppermost, over the top of the tee. Take the inside tool with right hand and place it in the crook so that the sharp end projects 2in (50mm) or so. The left thumb holds the tool down upon the armrest, and both of these down upon the tee. The fingers of the left grasp the pedestal of the tee rest, with the exception of the forefinger, which supports the crook from below. It is now easy to open the already bored hole with the inside tool. Although not essential, I often turn a groove at the bottom of the aperture, as shown below, using a handmade left-hand parting tool.

An annular groove will prevent the chaser striking the bottom of the aperture, and damaging the threads

This gives a useful clearance, preventing the chaser striking the bottom of the aperture and possibly damaging the threads.

I know the printed word cannot demonstrate the precise modus operandi any better than still photographs, so I can only say, experiment. Adjust the height and distance of the tee to what suits you. The tool can be raised or lowered by movement of the left shoulder up or down, or by holding the armrest handle a little lower down the side. The inside tool is moved independently upon the armrest, the same as it would be upon the tee. Far from being troublesome or awkward, the armrest is perfectly easy to master, giving extra accessibility and freedom of movement, to say nothing of wonderful tool control and support which the unaided, yet blameless tee, couldn't possibly provide. Furthermore, it is a famous and ancient tool of professionals. Mine has a thong so that I can wear it over my right shoulder for instant use: I'd feel undressed without it!

The same gentle speed of 200rpm or so, is used for striking inside threads. Once a good thread is cut, faster speeds can be used, as trials will prove.

Hold the inside chaser upon the armrest, just as described for the inside tool, pointing into the hole, parallel to the ground, teeth facing left. The preliminary movement of the chaser is best described as a series of horizontal ovals, starting from the outside, travelling into the hole and back. The armrest moves together with the chaser and, when striking, the oval movement is changed to the beginning of a spiral by giving the chaser handle a slight twist as the tool enters. This gives the teeth a slight upward movement as they traverse into the hole, and promotes easier striking and cleaner cutting.

But don't forget – the lightest of touches until the sound thread is established. Once well and truly struck, the thread is advanced and deepened with short, parallel strokes, carefully replacing the tool into the threads each time, a movement which will be automatic if the chaser is applied lightly. The threads, on arrival at a specific diameter, should not be further enlarged, but rather, used to guide the chaser into the aperture, cutting pressure only being applied when the chaser reaches the unfinished portion inside. I should mention that it is not necessary to note the ever-moving screw thread and mate the teeth into it at each stroke – it is all done by feel.

INTERNAL THREAD

Just as a flat tool was used on the external thread to reduce its diameter, leaving enough thread to guide the chaser, the same is done on the internal thread using the inside tool to adjust the diameter and parallelism, and following with the chaser to give a clean finish. The aperture is countersunk slightly, for easier entry of the external screw.

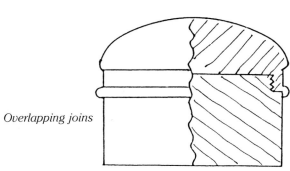

Overlapping joins

In order to get the hang of cutting inside screws, if you grip a plain ring of material, say about ⅝in (15mm) wide, in the three jaw chuck so that there is no bottom to impede the chaser, you'll find it twice as easy to cut a clean, true thread, and you'll feel with greater facility, how fast or slow the chaser should traverse. Each size of chaser needs a different

speed of traverse. A slow traverse on a coarse thread may give a double start thread, but you'll find your practice fascinating and rewarding.

For joining two parts with a screw, it is of small matter whether the inside or outside threads are cut first; usually it is the outside as it is easier to cut and measure, but it may be better to cut the inside threads first for some things, for example, when making a screwed box out of one piece of material. In any case, the internal thread is made a little longer to give clearance so the mating surfaces meet. The external threads on items which are to be frequently used are smoother in action and last longer if they are buff polished.

A drunk thread can cause an unsightly gap on one side of the mating surfaces which can only be rectified by making the screw a sloppy fit; this allows the surfaces to meet evenly at the expense of a firm fit. To avoid such bodged jobs it's a good plan to turn overlapping joins where possible so that unsightly gaps are hidden, as has been done in the sketch below. Hopefully, such drunk threads will be the

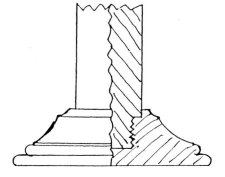

exception rather than the rule.

For anyone wishing to embark on the screw cutting adventure, a pair of chasers, 20 teeth per inch, would be my choice for a starting point. Once the facility has been properly mastered, a variety of sizes will undoubtedly be sought, but I never did like filling my jam jar with water until I'd caught my first fish!

Chapter 4 ● Tools *of the* BONE GRUBBERS

M y father, Bertram (1885-1969), had a wide experience in many kinds of turning. He gained this not only from his father and grandfather, who were also hardwood and ivory turners and carvers, but from his travels as a journeyman turner in London, Sheffield and Walsall. He was used to both treadle and power-driven lathes, and he started in business for himself in 1919, after being blown up at Passchendaele and

getting a handy 'blighty one'.

I was born in 1920, and my first memories of Bertram turning were in a coal cellar in Barret's Grove, Stoke Newington. He had a rough lathe with a crossover belt and large wooden treadle wheel. In those days one could fit up as a turner for a very few pounds: old headstocks and tailstocks could be bought in places like the Caledonian market – they even matched sometimes, sheer luxury! –

20

Above A typical assortment . . .

turning tools were made from penny files; taps, drills, screw tools and gouges were very cheap; benches were knocked up from old timber; and workshop rents were negligible.

The hardwood and ivory turner of the last century often had the largest diameter treadle wheel the bench could accommodate, and a very small pulley on the headstock. As the turner was no stranger to a 12 hour slog per day, maybe under a hot tin roof, it paid to get the maximum rotations per minute out of the energy he had to expend on his treadle. The belt (of gut or leather) lapped right round the mandrel pulley and crossed between the mandrel and the base of the headstock, as seen below, giving a non-slip drive.

Non-slip drive

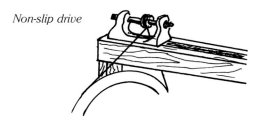

After a couple of years, Bertram moved to more spacious premises and employed six turners, including two brothers, turning mainly bone and horn shaving brush handles. I was always in the shop, of course, getting under everyone's feet. However, the landlord wanted the shop, so Bertram had to move after a few years. He took a much smaller workshop and employed only one turner, finding it more profitable, and less worrying than staggering under the load of six, not always very good, turners. We chucked the bone brush trade, and carried on with small bone, horn, ivory and hardwoods for all kinds of work.

EDUCATION

Three months before I was 14 – the official end of my obligation to attend school – Bertram said to me, 'How would you like to start work in the shop instead of wasting the last three months at school, learning nothing.' (An offer

not to be refused if ever I heard one!) Having got the three 'Rs' (especially the first two) well under my belt, I was all set to begin my real education, and started forthwith.

I'm afraid I was a very lazy boy, for as soon as Bertram's back was turned, I settled down to devour the *Magnet*, the *Gem*, and all the *Schoolboy's Own* Library, for which I heartily despised myself, and felt like Skinner of the Remove! In retrospect, however, my self-denigration has been tempered by the realization that such reading, even allowing for the essential 'Yarooh's' etc., more than compensated for my early retirement from school, where I wouldn't have learnt one-tenth of the Latin, Greek, Shakespeare and the classics that those splendid books gave me, and to which I added thereafter with further reading – and still do. In fact, my besetting sin of knocking off at the drop of a hat and settling down to read, has only been offset by the use of a record player and many LPs of Scottish dance or Vivaldi, etc., which urge my turning onwards with persistent gusto! Jimmy Shand is the repetition workers' foreman and pace-maker *par excellence*!

BONE AND HORN

I spent the next five years turning mainly bone and erinoid fittings for glass 'hit-and-miss' ventilators. When boiled and then kept moist, bone turns very well, but if attempted dry, it is too brittle and hard on the tools. Horn, which we

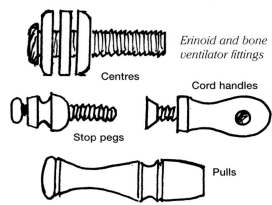

Erinoid and bone ventilator fittings

Centres

Cord handles

Stop pegs

Pulls

also used, is not soaked, but, as the grain tends to lift and flake, a chisel with a flat piece of spring steel (the type readily available from women's stays in those days!) tied on top works like a cabinet scraper and turns horn cleanly.

The pulls (four dozen an hour) are so simple to turn once you've got the knack – but that takes time. I can hear Bertram now as I'm making a disaster, 'Let me rescue that one!' – a deft sweep with a square tool, and in a second or two, perfection.

Now, although I became proficient at churning out the ventilator fittings etc., I considered myself more or less untrained when compared with Bertram, of whom I was very proud. You see, before WWI, bone grubbers, as hardwood and ivory turners were sometimes derisively called, were 'as thick as the leaves of Valembrosa' (numerically, not intellectually!), and although they lived reasonably, it was a hard working age, and those returning from the war either found that the trade was dying out (due to the onset of plastic materials, necessitated by the demise of so many craftsmen), or they had no desire to resume that work again themselves, or encourage their sons to do so.

RARITY

Bertram, in setting up in business as a hardwood and ivory turner, was a rarity, and his ability at turning and carving on the lathe was so attractive to me that I never had any other ambition but to follow the same line. In the 1920s there were dozens of hardwood and ivory turners, but over the next 20 years they faded out one by one like old soldiers, leaving no-one to follow. I found myself in the RAF for five jolly years in WWII, and on my return to civvy street, when I started my own turning shop in 1947, I was separated from Bertram by more than 100 miles (160km).

Having little practical experience in the wide variety of work he did, my confidence was poor, but he encouraged me by sending me work he knew I could do, and giving me full instructions for what was unfamiliar.

APPRENTICESHIP

In quite a short time I learned that my five-year 'apprenticeship' had given me all I needed in ability to handle everything that came my way. Of course, turning is not generally regarded as a romantic pursuit, so the lathe is widely regarded as an instrument of drudgery – but that image comes from the 'Dark Satanic Mills' days. It is almost unknown that some very famous people indeed, including royalty and many titled ladies and gentlemen of the last century, have pursued the art of turning in ivory and African blackwood on ornamental turning lathes, many of which were so superbly and handsomely constructed that they were sometimes used in the drawing room.

There is the story of the turner from Holtzapffel & Co. Lathemakers, calling at a great mansion to give His Lordship a turning lesson. The butler directed him to the tradesman's entrance: 'Tell your master,' replied the turner, 'that his master is here!'

But I knew nothing of all this because ornamental turning was outside the commercial sphere. In 1948, among some pieces I bought from an antiques dealer were two screwed ivory boxes that were ingeniously decorated in a way that was outside all my experience. Being ever on the qui vive for lathes and tackle, I met a dealer named Pike and showed him the boxes. He told me they were most likely made on a Howtzwissle lathe. He gave a brief description which interested me strangely, and said they were quite rare and costly, but he would keep an eye open for one. I never saw him again.

FAVOURITE LATHE

The lathes I used when I started my workshop were a big old 8in (203mm) head and tailstock with worn split bearings, and a 5in (127mm) hollow mandrel – not too good either! Both were mounted on the one bench, 12in (305mm) long, which I constructed with a large leg vice at one end. I had a length of shafting running underneath, with 10in (252mm), flat wooden pulleys to drive a back carriage behind each lathe, to provide foot-controlled variable speed. The belts were all 1in (25mm), flat leather that used to clack and jolt around the mandrel. Although very fine work was done, it couldn't always be described as comfortable. I kept my eyes open for improvements, however, and I soon got myself a brand new Acorn capstan headstock with Timken taper roller bearings, driven by vee belt. It cost £25 – not cheap 40 years ago – but it paid for itself in a month, finishing erinoid ball-point pens. It is still my favourite lathe.

The vee belt was such an improvement that I encouraged Bertram to make the change. He was delighted and we forthwith went over to vee belts, reserving the necessary flat ones for the slipping belt drive to the back carriages. Those happy days when I really began to enjoy my work produced a poem or two – we all have our weaknesses! By the way, a poem is never finished, but I've gone as far as I'm going with this one.

The Song of the Hardwood & Ivory Turner

It's the sweep o' the gouge from left to right & right to left again.
It's the bite o' the tool that's held just right & the curl o' the swarf again.
It's the tune o' the chaser biting deep & the smooth, crisp truth o' the screw.
It's the voice o' the screever parting off &, "another one less to do."
For the turners life is an active life, it's slash & cut all day.
If it's not your line better spend your time in a less exacting way.
But for them that'd stop in the turners shop for more than an hour or so,
And earn their meal with a turners steel in a trade where you daren't be slow,
It's the good old song o' the lathe again & the clack o' the belts below.

It's the rise & fall o' the restless hum as the mandrel changes speed,
It's the driving jolt o' the hammer's blow on the driven work & speed,
It's the sweat o' the ivory newly turned & the warm white kiss o' the flakes.
It's the sweep o' the square tool round a sphere & the firm, clean line it makes.
But don't you stop in the turners shop with a mind "whence all has fled,"
You must clear the way for the turners spray or the slap from an overhead.
You may crack your shin on a spare gear tin or your elbow against a rest,
But if you step in with a mind 'less dim on an honest, genuine quest,
It's a welcome true & a "how d'ye do!" & a yarn with one o' the best.

IVORY

Until comparatively recently, ivory was held in universal regard. Here's what I wrote on the subject a few years ago:

'Ivory is an emotive word today, yet it is a beautiful material that has been utilized for practical and decorative articles for as long as elephants have existed. Indeed, it is only the destruction of the majority of the world's craftsmen in two world wars that necessitated the plastic age of mass production. Before that time, everything used to be made of natural materials; wood, bone, horn, ivory, shells etc.

'Ivory has been collected for thousands of years – much of it stored and kept in good condition. There is swamp ivory, graveyard ivory, attic ivory, and "Aunty Flo's bit of ivory she's gonna sell for a bomb one day!" In Siberia, Alaska and other places, tons of mammoth ivory keep turning up, much of it well preserved in the ice. People have horded and prized this God-given substance from time immemorial, yet some well-meaning, misinformed souls are slandering and hurling abuse at anyone who possesses anything made of ivory. In many ways I do see their point, but the elephants who provided ivory for the vast majority of pieces one comes across have been dead for many years, often having died of old age. In order to retain sufficient vegetation to support the whole of the animal kingdom – including insatiable and ever-increasing man – in the regions where elephants live, it has ever been the practice to cull the herds, otherwise none would survive.

'Are we then, because of the lawless acts of some ruthless poachers, oft aided by avaricious governments, to destroy all goods made of ivory and persecute all who appreciate this material? How the ostracization of old ivory and goods made therefrom is going to preserve elephants is beyond my comprehension. I'm not about to end my days in a plastics factory!'

All is grist to the turner's mill and, apart from materials already mentioned, there are some ivory alternatives being produced now that are not only fair substitutes, but are a mere fraction of the price.

CHUCKS

The hardwood and ivory turner made nearly all his own chucks of boxwood or the like, chasing the mandrel nose thread for them with a chaser and armrest. Often he would even file up the chaser to fit the nose threads from a piece of steel or an old file – softened. He made chucks of all sizes – cup chucks into which the work was driven safely with a hammer. I use a 1½lb (680g) ball pein with a shortened handle. The good, slightly tapered end of the stock should fit about ⅛in (3mm) into the chuck, be well chalked, and then driven in with a calculated driving blow, not a shattering one. Rough it down with a gouge 'with a touch like a butterfly's wing', as Bertram used often to say, because it's the roughing operation that is most likely to de-chuck the work. Once that's done, all is pretty safe, though bad turning will jerk work out of almost any chuck – you'd better believe it. Turners have to be collectors of any and all unconsidered trifles – especially metal rings – because they're needed for all the wooden cup chucks, to prevent splitting.

Then there are boxwood arbors to accommodate grinding wheels, carving and roughing cutters, polishing mops, circular saws, sanding discs, driving prongs for woodturning, faceplates etc. – unlimited! Bertram also made his own small saw bench, using the tee rest pedestal. The saws were anything between 4–10in (100–250mm), and

of narrow gauge; 20–22 Standard Wire Gauge or stouter if required.

Self-centring chucks were used extensively, usually small, but could be up to 125mm. In them were turned all sorts of small work and rods of various materials. Drills, taps, carving cutters, etc., could also be clamped in SC chucks.

Usually there were turners and there were carvers, but a few contrived to do both, as Bertram did. The carving practised by turners was mostly done in the lathe, using all sizes and shapes of cutters, rotary files and burrs. It is not unusual to see selections in good toolshops, but many of the multifarious shapes and jobs that turn up may require something unobtainable, and these have to be home-made. All sorts of bits and pieces are utilized in making carving cutters – bolts of all sizes, even nails. I said your turner was a collector!

HUB CUTTER

To make a piece of stock fit a cup chuck, a large cutter, called a hub, was, and still is, used. This cutter is so valuable a tool for shaping all kinds of

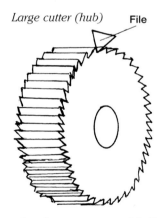

Large cutter (hub)   File

work, that even if carving is never envisaged, it is a must for every type of turner who values time. The exact measurements are not important, but I have drawn it full size, left. I can't resist interjecting at this point, that while at school my art master, Mr Gooch, so convinced me that I should never be any good at painting and drawing, that I was fool enough to put off trying for nearly 40 years – and they call that education!

To make such a tool, a blank disc of steel, drilled, and painstaking work filing about 10 teeth per inch (25mm) are needed. As a start, it would help a lot to use a hacksaw carefully, to make a cut about ¹⁄₁₆in (2mm) deep for every tooth. Simply file each tooth with a triangular saw file – I use a 10in (254mm) double ender – micrometers we do not possess on principle. Like the Cornish never really said, 'We don't work to the 10,000th part o' the inch, we d'work exzackly!'

If you keep one side of the file perpendicular, in radial line with the centre, as illustrated left, all will be well. Mild steel will retain its cut for years, so hardened steels you do not want. Of course, you'll make a boxwood chuck to screw on the mandrel nose as an arbor to mount the cutter (called a hub), with bolt, washer and nut. Mine is used at about 2,300 rpm. In use, the work is held and rotated against the hub, at around 7 o'clock.

Are you nervous at the notion of a bad gash from the whirling teeth? Well, once I had a cutter of hardened steel, beautifully sharpened. It didn't take long ere it snatched and made a small vee cut on a finger. I'd been too clever. The old timers filed their cutters out of mild steel, and they weren't too sharp so they didn't snatch. I removed that cutter, softened it, and have felt better ever since.

A cutter that isn't too sharp will allow you to touch it lightly without fear, but if you force the work, instead of allowing the tool to do the cutting, you will risk a slip which may break the skin a leetle – not a lot! And of course, if your lathe is under foot control, your ability to stop or slow down in a trice will vastly increase confidence. Hold the work down and it can't snatch. Remember that, and give yourself time to practise until you learn exactly what you can and can't do with the hub. It's so easy to be put off using good tools, so never let the 'Mr Goochs' put you off. I tell you – any kid in the street can do it!

If you start carving it is surprising how much can be done with this cutter alone. There is plenty of scope for the small cutters to carve the detail, but only after the work has been roughed to shape with the hub. As a start, take any old piece of wood and try. Do not have the tee rest or any other impediments too close – this is freehand. Keep your fingers clear as you hold and move the wood against the hub, at the aforesaid 7 o'clock. If the wood drags against it, there can be no snatch. Take a square-ended piece and hub it round with a slight taper to fit a cup chuck. You may pencil a circle on the bottom as a guide if you wish. You will soon be familiar with its ways and wonder how the dickens you managed without it before. When I was a kid I did this for years, hubbing small bone to fit iron chucks. It has to be a good fit – if it isn't, the piece may come out just when you've cut a long screw on it.

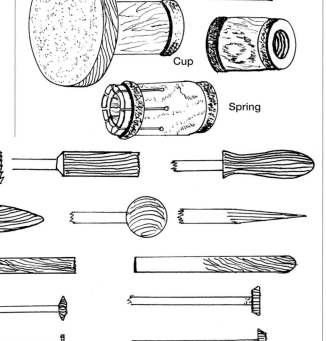

Various chucks and cutters

Chapter 5 ● Chucking METHODS *and* Ornamental TURNING

*L*et me take you through a precise piece of turning in African blackwood or boxwood, that calls for patience and step-by-step accuracy. It is a set of bishops, and the accuracy is called for because the four should be alike when they are all compared. We aren't using 'mikes', so we have a trifle of tolerance and reasonableness, having regard to the fact that it is hand work. Indeed, the late Edward Pinto – famous for 'Treen' (both the book and the vast collection) – told me when I apologized for the slight discrepancy in some restoration work I was doing for him, 'Ah. It is the small discrepancies that constitute the charm of hand work'. Good old Pinto – he restores one's faith in human nature!

However experienced, chucking methods will always exercise the brain. Some are obvious, but others offer a choice: 1 Easy; 2

Possible; 3 What you can hope to get away with. If I used a cup chuck I could get away with it, but for this I'll use a 4in (100mm), self-centring, four jaw, geared scroll, then I only have to saw the blackwood into square lengths, chuck by one end, and turn the other

Blackwood and ivory chess set

end nice and parallel, then reverse and chuck it firmly by the turned end.

Nobody likes heavy, great jaw chucks whirling at great speed, but many other things

27

Left *Holtzapffel headstock (No. 1848 – the Eldorado)*

we have to endure in life are far more dangerous: we simply learn to respect them, do what we can to mitigate them, and then use them carefully. In the case of jaw chucks, variable speed foot control gives increased confidence, but there is a useful dodge that everyone can do to overcome the worst snag, and that is to round off the sharp, leading outer edges and corners of the jaws – both inner and outer sets – on the grindstone. This will save sundry lacerations – you may depend on it!

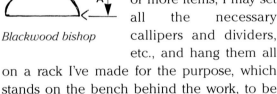

Blackwood bishop

As you will see from the sketch, left, I have marked 10 diameters with arrows, and eight distances with lines; every turner will have personal preferences for measuring. For a dozen or more items, I may set all the necessary callipers and dividers, etc., and hang them all on a rack I've made for the purpose, which stands on the bench behind the work, to be instantly to hand. You'll laugh, but it took more

than half a century for me to devise this method, after a lifetime of grubbing about among the shavings, tools, and bric-a-brac on the bench, looking for callipers and things. Now, I take them down from the rack in order – and hopefully, I remember to replace them! If I am making only four items though, I will sometimes use only one vernier calliper (a good old Mauser picked up at an auction sale and repaired), and reset it for every measurement as it comes up. It works fine for me and saves time.

Screever – side view

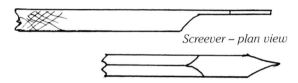

Screever – plan view

Turn parallel with a ⅜in (10mm) light gouge, and surface end. Measure and mark length, and cut in with screever about 1⁄16in (2mm) deep. Turn down to largest diameter – the base – finishing cleanly with the square tool. Turn the rest down to the next largest diameter, just above A, and clean up that specific part with the square tool. Turn down to next diameter, the flange just above C, and clean that part too.

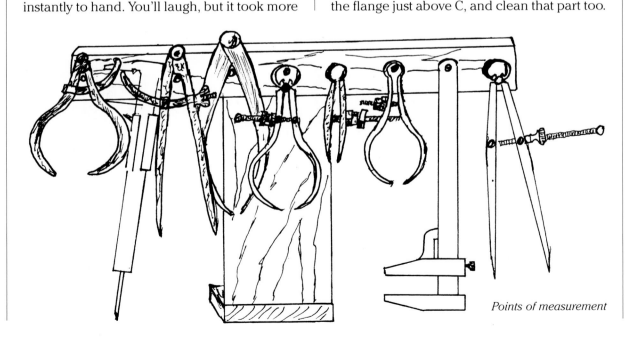

Points of measurement

Three square file – point tool

We take our measurement and mark the top of the flange below the ball, and make a vee cut with the point tool.

Next, turn end down to slightly larger than the ball diameter. As you measure the diameter of ball, also mark its length and mark with a pencil midway to give you the centre of the ball.

We'll turn this next, using the long-handled, ³⁄₁₆in (4mm), round nose tool. I use three square files, but then, I use anything that works well, and this little file does. When roughing down hard materials that a large tool might fetch out of the chuck, the positive cut of such a small tool in a long handle, firmly held, but lightly applied, really achieves a beautiful cut, superbly controlled.

A word on controlling the tool. You may recall, if you saw the film *Scaramouche*, that Perigal, the great Parisian fencing master, gave this instruction for holding the grip of the sword or foil . . . 'hold it as you would hold a bird, not so as to crush it, yet not in any event to allow it to escape'. Tools handled with finesse a la Monsieur Perigal are less likely to de-chuck the work, or snap through violence.

Back to the ball (as M'lady said). Having roughed it fairly round, always taking great care not to turn away wood you will need (and you won't do that unless you are in undue haste), finish it as nearly as possible by eye, with the square tool sweeping round upon the armrest – a must for this job – and the point tool.

The perfect ball is finished by the use of a steel tube of slightly smaller diameter than that of the ball. The tube (overall length about 4in (100mm), including handle, if necessary), is

Sharpened tube for ball turning

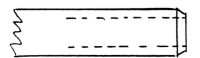

gripped in the self-centring chuck, and opened to the right inside diameter, i.e. about ¹⁄₁₆in (1.5mm) smaller than the ball diameter, with an inside tool on the armrest. Make it conical at the end but not sharp, like the one shown below left.

The best results are obtained by rubbing an India stone across the front, while the lathe is running slowly, then finishing by just touching again with the inside tool. If frequently sharpened in the same manner, hardened steel is not essential. Tubes of assorted sizes accumulate, so that the longer one is a turner, the larger and more extensive grows the stock of accoutrements. Some of my tools, cutters, tubes etc., are even made of brass because it happened to be handy at the time – and it does the job, so why not?

Pencil the ball all over, run the lathe quite slowly, then, with the tube resting on the tee, move it over the ball from left to right and back again gently, until it clears the pencil marks evenly. Don't use force or it may burn. The tube is one of those simple tools which, judiciously used, make for perfection.

To finish Part D, turn down the tiny bead next to the ball to the right diameter, and finish with the point tool. The sweep up to the edge of the flange is done with another small file tool.

A small file tool can be put to many uses

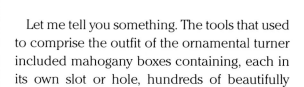

Let me tell you something. The tools that used to comprise the outfit of the ornamental turner included mahogany boxes containing, each in its own slot or hole, hundreds of beautifully finished edge tools for slide rest, cutting frames, drill spindle etc. The proud owner of same has a magic box of tricks that will, in the right hands (and therein lies the catch), accomplish many marvels, because each tool can be used in socket handles, with a small thumb screw to tighten. Of course, it is unashamed luxury, as only one-tenth of them were ever used.

Tradesmen never aspired to such feather-bedding, which is the reason so many files were used to make what was needed.

Part C is turned next, with tools shaped like those shown right, and a point tool. Part B is plain sailing with gouge and ½in (12mm) round tool. Part A is left till last for the obvious reason that the narrow neck, if turned first, would make the piece too weak to stand up to the tooling.

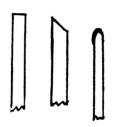

Three small file tools, with different shapes for different tasks

APPLIED PRECISION

All tooling for this careful work is done with applied precision. The small tools are carefully manipulated at very low lathe speeds, feeling your way, as it were, so that any tendency to rib, chatter or dig in is automatically counteracted by the foot control. I was sent an old chesspiece to copy very recently, by a turner who said the grooves – they were about ⅛in (3mm) and extremely deep – were so narrow, he broke a tool trying and gave up. With variable speed, you can ease the tool in gently, clearing as you go, and if it starts to bind, simply slow down instantly and clear it before the inevitable happens. Variable speed can't solve every problem, but of a certainty, it is the beginner's best friend.

Tools are applied so that as the required shape emerges, it is finished with the wood shiny and cleanly turned. This may require varying lathe speeds, which one can only sense by experience – just like car gears. There may still be striae, slight tool marks, so work is well sanded with 'old fine'. Indeed, the old Sheffield turners used to say the best turner in the trade was John Oakey (he's the glasspaper maker!).

In Chapter 4 I mentioned two decorated screwed boxes, and my interest in how they were made. All I knew about ornamental turning was that plain turned work held stationary in the lathe was further worked upon by instruments held in a slide rest and driven by an overhead gear. I might have gone on pondering forever had it not been for the demise of my boxwood catheter plug trade, when such things were replaced by plastic. This caused me to offload a stock of boxwood offcuts in postal parcels by advertising in *The Woodworker*. One of the replies came from Albert Kelly, a fellow devotee of the lathe, and when he called to see me, he was able to throw some light on ornamental turning.

SOCIETY OF ORNAMENTAL TURNERS

Two years before, in 1948, the late Fred Howe, the great master turner and carver, with several others who were concerned at the rapid decline of all knowledge of ornamental turning, founded the Society of Ornamental Turners, with the aim of preventing its complete demise, and ensuring that as many as possible of the wonderful old ornamental turning outfits were not flogged off to the scrap merchants or consigned to the murky depths of a museum basement. The Society would try to re-open the world of ornamental turning before it vanished utterly, simply because so very few had any knowledge of its existence.

Well, my family had been turners as far back as we could remember and knew nothing of it! Why? Easy. Ornamental turning wasn't a trade – it was a diversion for the wealthy. It was the elite way of turning and shaping and decorating choice materials, using sophisticated, complex, but clean and delightful machinery which could be, and sometimes was, used in the drawing room by ladies as well as gentlemen. Then the motor car was invented, and they all went out to enjoy life in other ways. Their lathes went in all directions, as we know by the present owners, and the

Society keeps a fatherly eye on as many as it has knowledge of.

Albert, who had joined the new Society of Ornamental Turners, gave me particulars, so I forthwith applied to the Honorary Secretary, Fred Howe, who sent me details and an invite to the next Society meeting. I was always a breezy character, sticking my chin out and throwing my hat in the ring, and I thought it highly unlikely that an amateur would find it very easy to make a 7in (175mm), two-piece ivory cigarette holder. I had found it a bit difficult myself at first so, playfully, I challenged Fred to make a tube, and I sent him a sample.

Until then I had led a sheltered life, knowing nothing about ornamental turning and the work done by amateurs. The amateur can be surprising and, with time and enthusiasm, can achieve miracles. He can't usually compete with the professional, but of course, that is not his aim.

THE brotherhood of the lathe must be almost unique in friendly encouragement

At that first meeting, you could have knocked me down with a motor jack! Well, what a marvellous gang they were in those days! Many legendary turners were alive at that time and they gave me a hearty welcome, and praised my poor efforts too – for all were encouraged to bring work. The brotherhood of the lathe must be almost unique in friendly encouragement. Dear Fred had, of course, made a couple of two-piece tubes impeccably – and ornamented them! I saw many marvels that day.

Thereafter, Fred and I visited each other. He had access to much equipment, and very soon he made me an exciting offer of . . . 'enough equipment to do all the ornamental turning

you'll want, for £25'. It consisted of a division plate, an ornamental slide rest, an overhead gear, and three cutting frames (eccentric, horizontal and vertical).

HOLTZAPFFEL

Before I could convert one of my lathes for ornamental turning use, another member sold me a Holtzapffel headstock and tailstock. The headstock was a 5in (125mm) back-centre type with division plate and index, and some members said I'd been 'done', when I paid £20 for it! I constructed a stout, rough timber bench, fitted two lengths of 1½in (38mm) angle iron to the top for the head and tailstocks to rest on, and spent a couple of days filing it flat. I fitted the overhead gear and motorized the lathe in my usual way, but extending the variable speed to the overhead gear. It worked perfectly!

Yet again, I'd scarcely begun when a better head and tailstock came up for auction. This one was a Holtzapffel and Deyerlein, with traversing mandrel for screw cutting. It was made in 1813 and sold new and complete for £136 –it's in the Holtzapffel ledger. It cost me £9 10s, and I fitted it to my new bench, and offloaded my first Holtzapffel for goods to the value of £20. The buyer also felt he'd been done – but not now. He knows it was worth every penny!

ENTER THE VAMPIRE

So – imagine me sitting in my lovely workshop in DeBeauvoir town, London, listening to the test commentary one afternoon in the early 1950s, when a knock came on the door and in walked a peculiar little man. His face must have been all but destroyed by fire, although repaired as well as possible: one ear was absent and he wore one black glove.

He was a Scot with a corncrake voice, and he was seeking work as a toolmaker at an engineering firm whose whereabouts he hoped I might know. He was in no hurry to leave, so I proudly showed him my lathes and my work. He asked if I was making a good living and I assured him my business was on a very solid foundation – the rocks!

I was eloquent on the subject of ornamental turning, although having to admit it was hardly likely to be a commercial success. 'I enjoy pottering with it at odd times', I told him. Having had a good innings, he asked if I'd care to hear some helpful suggestions. Permission being granted he began to speak, quietly at first, but gradually working up to a fine, loud flow of oratory, like a public speaker, slapping his gloved fist into his palm from time to time and drawing his breath in with a hissing sound. The gist of it was this: my shop was 50 years behind the times a museum piece now! – and there was I, laboriously making things by hand and wasting my time with trash! Here he indicated the *Radio Times* and my ornamental lathe; 'Do you know what that is?', his voice took on a sinister note as his gloved fist pointed darkly at my beloved lathe, 'It's a vampire', he bared his teeth and hissed, 'A vampire, and it's sucking your blood – get rid of it!'.

He then went on to explain how we could make our fortune! Starting with an empty shop we should buy a fly-press and go into the high class tin toy business. He had all the plans, but no capital, so he went on his way and I was left with much food for thought. . . Did I want a fortune? No! Did I wish to press poor harmless flies? Not especially. And what was the test score? I was back to normal, but from that day on my Holtzapffel and Deyerlein lathe has been called the Vampire.

THE WORKINGS OF THE VAMPIRE

For the benefit of those on my wavelength I must describe the Vampire, as it is rather a mouthwatering contraption, and quite practical if anyone did fancy making it. Better

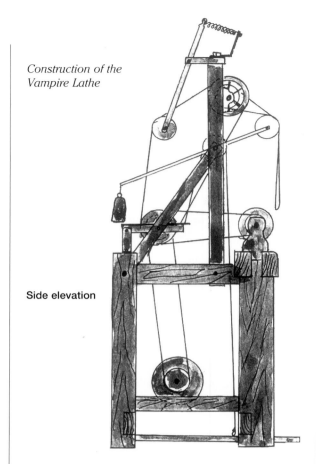

Construction of the Vampire Lathe

Side elevation

still, it is good fun for any lathe enthusiast to contemplate.

The overhead standards, back carriage, and motor supports are all angle iron. The 4in (100mm) flat pulley on the motor (I turned mine in hardwood) drives the same sized flat pulley on the back carriage via a 1in (25mm) flat leather belt. The wooden triple pulley on the back carriage is turned to the sizes to suit your needs. In my case the left and right vee pulleys are 6in (150mm). There is a hardwood spindle and the pulley is recessed for inset ballraces of about 2⅜in (60mm) diameter – it is not important, but you certainly never buy new ones! If you make slots in the sides of the angle iron you will be able to adjust the spindle to alter the belt tension.

The left hand vee pulley drives the headstock (either by round leather or vee belt), and it receives its drive from the afore-mentioned flat belt, from the motor. The

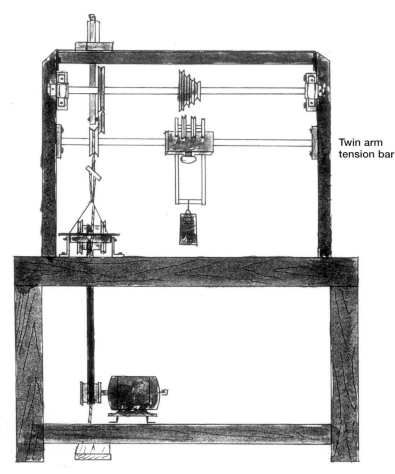

Twin arm
tension bar

Back carriage plan

Front, with lathe
omitted for clarity

hinged back carriage is raised and lowered by the foot pedal, which has an adjuster on the cord. To arrive at the exact length of the flat belt, the tension is such that when the back carriage is fully raised, the foot hard down, and the belt quite taut, the front of the back carriage angle iron is exactly midway between the lathe driving belt, as depicted in the side elevation shown above left.

Unless the pedal is depressed, the flat belt is too slack to drive, so any speed from nought to maximum can be obtained in seconds – forget your switches! Judge, ye chatterers, how easy is the remedy when you can do this, and how you can vary the speed automatically for differing diameters on the same piece of work, to say nothing of the essential facility of variable speed for hand screw-cutting.

I always hated a direct drive on the overhead. I like my eccentric cutter to pause a while when I adjust the index. It can do with a

rest, and I do not relish the thing whirring so close to my nose! Also, I like to run it at a controlled speed, which helps to improve the cutting perfection in varying circumstances.

So, the overhead is driven by the right hand pulley with a round leather belt. In this case, the upward movement of the back carriage necessitates a sprung jockey pulley to take up the slack. It works like a charm! Lathe and overhead can be run together or separate, and performance is excellent. I have made a twin arm tension bar so that it does not foul the top pulley when raised high as necessary. Some overheads have their shafting too near the front of the lathe, but I have set mine 8in (200mm) behind the headstock and that seems ideal. Don't worry if you don't understand everything yet – 'tis a big subject! Everything will fall into place, but mark this, ornamental turning is most assuredly not for the impatient.

Chapter 6 ● The *Ornamental* Turners' SLIDE REST

*A*re any two turners alike? I don't know of any. Each turner works in ways that differ from all the others, maybe slightly, maybe completely, and one type of turning differs from another. Softwood turning was not usually practised by the hardwood and ivory turners: the softwood turner makes articles of a useful, general domestic nature, while the hardwood and ivory turner covers the elaborate side, and works quite differently. Although some may have costly apparatus, most use simple means to produce work that may be extremely complex. Results that would seem to demand expensive tools are often achieved by ingenuity and skill.

Above Turning a king's stem with ¼in (6mm) gouge

Some turners are fortunate in having a wide range of experience, covering both soft and hardwood, ivory, bone and metal. Few can succeed with all of these as well as the turner who devotes his whole attention to one branch only. Some ornamental turners are accomplished model and tool makers who enjoy making apparatus for their lathes far more than actually using it when completed (in some cases it would probably bore them).

There are some masters – you could count them on one hand now – who are not only wizards in the engineering workshop, but also in turning incredible ornamental pieces, using a great deal of the complicated equipment in Holtzapffel Volume 5: I doubt if any one person possesses the whole of it.

My own approach to ornamental turning has been through hand turning. The lathe to me has ever been a means to an end – of accomplishing the work in hand in the most efficacious manner. If it can be done by skill of hand, that is how I do it, providing the slide rest would not make the result infinitely superior. If not, I will not waste time with apparatus.

This, I am sure, makes me less skilled in the mechanical side of ornamental turning, but I feel that with hand and machine I have the best of both worlds: of course, any and everyone who produces good work on the ornamental turning lathe has got to be useful with his or her hands – it is, emphatically, not simply winding a few handles!

The ornamental turning purist might consider my work inferior to the wholly machine-made item, but there is, fortunately, no war between the two schools. Indeed, there is mutual admiration, for if the hand turner has greater manual dexterity, the machine turner probably has superior knowledge, especially in maths.

I read a magazine article describing a turner – world famous of course – who, apparently becoming hooked on Holtzapffel's volumes, bought a super-duper ornamental turning outfit, religiously copied all the designs of the Master (that I would have to see), and became disenchanted. Why? 'Because,' it said, 'he began to question the value of such arid, stereotyped work.' He forthwith put up the shutters on ornamental turning, and tried elsewhere as it were.

There are ornamental turners of many kinds, and I for one would be proud and delighted to 'aridly stereotype' a modest tenth of the works in question, had I the brains. In truth, we can never copy any piece of ornamental turning exactly, however hard we try. The scope for variety and sheer ingenuity shrieks 'sour grapes' at the use of such outre terms to describe the beloved art of ornamental turning.

IF the hand turner has greater manual dexterity, the machine turner probably has superior knowledge, especially in maths

Of course, many examples of ornamental turning are perhaps an acquired taste. By the same token, we all know poor examples of plain turnery, but never should we condemn any reputable art form though we may criticize the artist. If the work is arid, blame the turner, plain or ornamental.

My purpose is to enjoy turning in the various ways open to me, in whatever time I can make. I've been through some of the books on ornamental turning and reflected on what a complicated subject it can be. Most of them arouse my keen interest and teach me so much, that I have come to the conclusion that

I know next to nothing about complex ornamental turning or engineering.

I am like Winston Churchill when he began painting. He started late in life and hadn't any time for all the preliminary training and practice. There he was in front of a large white canvas and, having nervously made a mark the size of a bean upon that affronted sheet, he saw a lady he knew approaching. That got him going. Slam, bang, wallop!, and that painting was well underway on the now cowering canvas.

Of course, we can't do that with ornamental turning, but we can pick it up to an extent as we go along. 'Everything comes to him who waits', said Bertram and added, 'if you don't die while you're waiting.' 'Tis a pretty art to contemplate while so doing.

Fred Howe, co-founder of the Society of Ornamental Turners, said you can do all the ornamental turning you'll want with a division plate, a slide rest, some cutting frames, and an overhead gear. I have no criticism of ornamental work that is extravagant, leaving very little of the material undecorated. If a really good turner thoroughly enjoyed making it, I will probably enjoy the piece too. On the other hand, I don't like using machinery 'because it's there', and for no other reason. Being a hand turner, my chief joy is to make the shapes I want (as opposed to hoping they'll look reasonable when I've finished work with the tools), and quite often, very little or no further embellishment seems called for.

BASIC EQUIPMENT

To start with the basics, what is needed? 1 Division plate and index; 2 Ornamental slide rest; 3 Overhead gear; and 4 Cutting frames (eccentric, vertical, horizontal, drilling spindle). The brass division plate shown in the photo has three rows of holes; 360, 144, and 112. The last two are usually sufficient for me,

but were I making a plate I'd plump for 180, 144, 120, 112, and 96. You can't drill such holes using dividers and a centre punch. A master plate is needed and a ⅟₃₂in (1mm) centre drill.

The index can be a piece of stiff, flat spring with a pointer set in its upper end, nicely made to fit the holes. At its base is fitted a

Holtzapffel headstock

tapered pin which passes through a hole in a spherical boss, which is screwed either into the base of the headstock or just below, into the bench itself.

In the photo above, you can see that the index is adjustable, as it finishes with a screw and two knurled nuts which can raise or lower

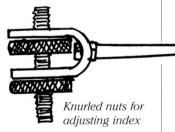

Knurled nuts for adjusting index

the index in cases where the start of a pattern is not compatible with a hole, but falls between two, or where work has to be removed, and of course it's pounds to pancakes the holes won't line up with the pointer, except by adjustment.

Behind the division plate, you'll see a worm-wheel and tangent screw which ends in a small pulley (for slow drive from the overhead) and a square end to the spindle for a winch handle. A series of graduated collars can be slipped on the square-ended spindle immediately in front of the pulley. The worm-wheel has 180 teeth, and with the aid of the collars, any number of divisions can be made when the tangent screw is raised into mesh with the worm-wheel – a valuable asset for cutting clock wheels. In fact, in Holtzapffel Volume 5 (page 438) appears a tangent table giving the collars together with the exact number of turns of the winch handle to obtain divisions of the circle, from 2 to 8,280: can you beat that?

Segment apparatus

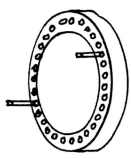

The 76 larger holes that circumambulate the worm-wheel are used with the vertical bar alongside, and constitute a piece of apparatus known as 'the segment plate and stops' or the 'segment engine' (which sounds vastly superior).

The stop carries two capstan-headed adjusting screws closely adjacent to the holes which are for the purpose of inserting two taper pins in pre-arranged locations. When the mandrel is turned, either by hand or tangent screw, these pins, coming in contact with heads of the screws, confine its rotation to strict limits which can be finely adjusted by screwing or unscrewing the capstan-headed screws.

This apparatus, especially when used with ornamenting chucks such as eccentric, recti-linear, or spherical, is capable of shaping and producing surface patterns limited only by the little grey cells of the turner.

SLIDES

In the view of the ornamental slide rest below, there is a main slide with a top slide and one fluting stop. The thick column which fits into the slide rest pedestal has alongside it, a smaller, round bar, one of a pair, fitted to an arc of steel, and attached to the underside of the main slide. These bars abut against projections on the pedestal, which are accurately adjusted by horizontal screws passing through them as shown below.

Main slide

Pedestal with brass elevating ring. This can be screwed up or down and clamped to give the precise height of centre required

The movement of the main slide when it is turned round in the circular fitting of the pedestal is limited, and it can only move between the points of the adjusting screws. When the pedestal is exactly at right angles to the lathe bearers, the screws are adjusted so that the one brings the mainslide parallel with the mandrel axis, and the other at right angles to it. The mainslide can, of course, be fixed at any intermediate angle, and the best slide rests are equipped with a quadrant plate and pointer for trouble-free accuracy. As the

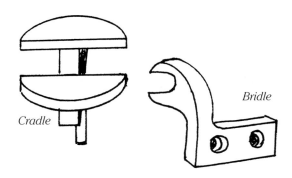

Cradle

Bridle

1 A fluting stop. These fit on the mainslide, on each side of the top slide, at any required distance, to determine the exact length of the traverse of the tool.
2 Small key with square hole.
3 Tool receptacle, which fits into the top slide, with drilling spindle and two clamping screws. Note the long screws on both sides of the receptacle: the nearer is the depth stop (which butts against the small column on the top slide), and the further is the guide screw.
4 Operating lever. The hole fits over the rear clamping screw and the slot over the left or right upright column on the top slide, whichever is convenient.

pedestal is also housed in a 'cradle' which fits exactly between the lathe bearers, the pedestal is always at perfect right angles to them, so that accuracy with simplicity is assured.

The parts listed here can be seen in the photo on page 37, from the rear, below the mainslide:

Slide rest, minus tool receptacle

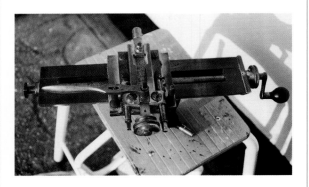

Main slide with drill spindle clamped and operating lever in position

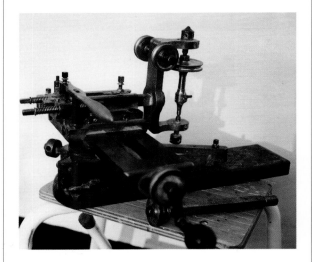

Horizontal cutting frame set-up

Eccentric cutting frame set-up

I mentioned the depth stop to the left of the tool receptacle and the guide screw on the right in the eccentric cutting frame, shown bottom right. Immediately behind the graduated collar at the end of the guide screw is a recessed portion 1⁄4in (6mm) wide: a bridle can be screwed to the right hand double-bevel bar (you can see the two screws in the photo) so that the tool can only be advanced by key or winch handle on the guide screw. The operating lever cannot be used with the bridle in position.

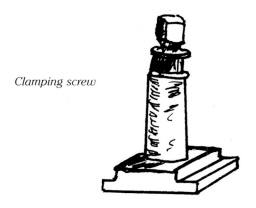

Clamping screw

Apart from cutting frames, the receptacle can accommodate gouge and chisel cutter bars and heavy tools with square section shanks that fill the receptacle. Also, a large selection of small, slide rest tools, about 3 x ⅜ x ⅛in (75 x 9 x 3mm), are used with a filling piece below and a clamping bar on the top, recessed to fit over the tool. The three-piece 'sandwich' is secured as are the cutting frames by the two clamping screws. The valuable asset of all these tools is that, once the slide rest is set to the correct height of centre, all tools will be at the same height.

It must be noted that the ornamental turning slide rest is for fine and delicate work, and while it is used for plain turning before any decorating is done, excessive demands which might impair or damage it are best avoided: rougher turning to reduce material to shape should be done by hand turning. There is a metal slide rest for heavier work, but as afore-mentioned, I am a hand turner and seldom do plain work with the slide rest.

Having described, very briefly, the ornamental turning slide rest, it has to be said that they are not easy to come by. Even in the Society of Ornamental Turners they are not items easy to separate from their owners, but at least you keep in touch with tools and information unknown elsewhere. Many turners have either made their own tools or adapted engineers' lathes to perform some delightful ornamental work. After all, who in these days would want – or could put up with – the whole range?

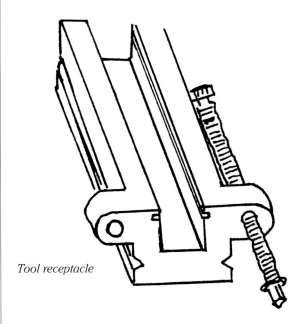

Tool receptacle

The main slide is usually 13 x 2⅝in (330 x 66mm). The covered leading screw is 10 teeth per inch, with a winch handle at one end. It passes through a nut beneath the top slide, by which it can be traversed in either direction. The tool receptacle is like an open-ended box which accepts the (normally) ⁹⁄₁₆in (14mm) square cutting frames, secured by two clamping screws which slide in horizontal grooves in the sides of the receptacle. The collar on the depth stop and screw guide is graduated, and a mark is engraved on the top of the stop (on the top slide) to read against the head of the screw.

Chapter 7
Overhead GEARS

*A*s I have emphasized in previous chapters, ornamental turning is not for the impatient, and is very seldom found in trade circles, as its devotees are fired by love of the pursuit. It has never been a commercial proposition, although at least one high class firm did produce notable work in the first half of the last century, but even for those not personally inclined to acquire the items that would enable them to enjoy a moderate range of ornamental turning, there is a fascination in reading about it (provided its many complexities are never permitted to become wearisome). My brain automatically switches off when this happens, so don't worry – I am a simple dabbler in ornamental turning. Further, I do not like targets, so if some genius produces five

40

Above *A tidy workshop . . .*

wafer thin, hollow boxwood balls, all inter-linked, and some other genius tries to write down exactly how it was done, unless this can be followed successfully, I echo my grand-father's words, 'Very nice old cock, but can you earn a living at it?'

Whatever anyone else has done superla-tively, I do not do. I think it's always best to be yourself and aim for a measure of originality. Complete originality is all but impossible, but it's the personal touches of adaptation that ring the bell.

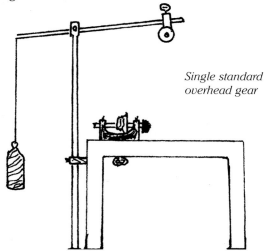

Single standard overhead gear

Many have been put off ornamental turning by so many glaring examples of over-embell-ished kitsch – bad art, where the fault is not in the tackle, but the turner – and there have been, and still are, some really splendid exponents of the art. For those who are seriously interested, have a mathematical turn of mind and a determination to understand the principles, then Holtzapffel, Volume 5 is a must, and will give you the unequivocal answer to the question, 'to be, or not to be an ornamental turner'. With this 'bible' you will not need excessive details from me, but will be able to decide if this form of addiction is what you've been looking for. For those who aren't, yet, aiming to go so far, a little knowledge of how it works should be of interest because, with even a few modifications, a plain turner

can equip himself with additional abilities that will expand his potential and double his enjoyment of his art.

Now, to the overhead gear. The one on my Vampire lathe (see Chapter 5) is excellent, but many other arrangements may be used. Unless heavy work, such as milling, is envisaged, a single standard situated to the left of the lathe bench will be ideal. A stout length of iron pipe 72 x 1¼in (1,830 x 32mm), clamped to the left side of the bench just behind the lathe, should have a slotted fork to support a swinging arm, fitted loosely into the top so that it can turn freely. At one end of the arm a weight, 4.4–6.6lb (3–4kg), is suspended. Along the other end is an adjustable block carrying twin pulleys which can be fitted to the arm fore and aft, or sideways if required.

The materials used for making any equipment are of little importance: as long as it is strong enough to do the job, wood may stand in for metal. Some people can turn out marvellous work with what would appear to be rubbish. You know it is often thus – the kids with rubbishy, home-made tackle caught the fish, while poor old Sid Mundy, who spent a fortune on the finest fishing tackle money could buy, and went fishing to escape the bitter tongue of a shrewish wife, seldom got a bite. He enjoyed it though, and that's the main thing.

IMPROVISER

The turner should always be a great improviser, ever on the qui vive for oddments of metal, lengths of angle iron, piping, brackets, nuts, bolts, springs, washers, pulleys of all types, ad infinitum. So you won't need to ask me what pulleys to use on the swinging arm – use whatever comes your way. I found some lovely fibre ones with inset ball races, but wood or metal are both good, as long as they have nice, deep vees and spin freely. With the grand-daddy of all machine tools, the lathe, there is very little that cannot be contrived if the turner sets his mind to it, especially if he is friendly with an engineer, a blacksmith, and a welder!

Were I at the beginning of my career instead of the end, I would make room for a Myford Super Seven or similar engineer's screw-cutting lathe, and thus be equipped to make some of the tools that are now scarce. Yet, without such valuable assets I have got by either awaiting them to fall into my lap – and they often have – or done without them. I must also weigh in the balance the certain fact that had I thus divided my time between hand turning and engineering, it would doubtless have been at the cost of some other skill, one way or t'other.

HOME-MADE OVERHEAD GEAR

Returning to our overhead gear, a small motor will be required – ⅙ or ⅛hp, 1,400RPM will be ideal. The motor is not bolted down, but stands freely on the bench wherever suitable for the work in hand. If a thick pad of sponge rubber or foam is placed beneath it, you will find it will drive positively and sweetly.

Make a wooden pulley for the motor; three steps, with the vees from 2–5in (50–125mm) (not critical). The ⅛in (3mm) leather, gut, cotton rope or polycord belt runs from the motor pulley over the twin pulleys on the swinging arm, and down to the cutting frame, the left hand weight providing the tension. The slotted fork is a loose fit in the upright standard, so the arm can be swivelled at will. The belt length is adjustable by moving the motor to wherever it is most effective.

Originally I had an arrangement where the motor was on a small platform at the left end of the swinging arm, and the motor provided the tension weight. You can say that again! When the thin leather belt broke, the motor crashed down with nerve-shattering abruptness, although no damage was done. I ditched that arrangement when I found a pair of fine

Evans' overhead standards, which I used to make a variable speed set-up like the Vampire. I also ditched leather for spliced cotton rope, and have had no breaks since.

Christie's the auctioneers have occasional sales of ornamental turning lathes and equipment, and while a long purse will be needed for the former, often the small, but vital items – cutting frames, slide rests, tools, etc. – have been known to go at affordable prices. Good, obsolete tools are worth whatever value you, the buyer, place on them.

The drilling instrument
(Holtzapffel Volume 5)

We're going to deal with the drilling instrument now. The drilling instrument is a square bar – usually ⁹⁄₁₆in (14mm) to fit the normal tool receptacle on the ornamental slide rest – which is bored to receive the spindle, which runs in hardened steel collars, coned-out and made so beautifully that I can vouch, they never wear out if kindly used. Should looseness occur, the slack can be taken up by a turn of the nut behind the pulley. The drills are individually made and turned *in situ*, fitting a tapered socket, giving complete accuracy when revolving in its own spindle. The business end is filed down to the diametrical line, precisely, to provide the cutting face.

KEEPING A SHARP EDGE

Perfection of cutting depends on the preservation of that diametrical status, so no sharpening should be done on the face, apart from a rub on an Arkansas oilstone (pronounced 'Arkensaw') to remove any burr raised while sharpening. Hollow drills, beadcutters, astragal cutters, double-quarter cutters, etc., are sharpened on brass cones run in the lathe, and dressed with fine grinding paste.

Ornamental turning is a perfectionist's art so of course, our scrupulously discriminating purist will say, 'Ah, but when using a revolving cone to sharpen a hollow tool, the leading half will, by virtue of the pressure and the one way thrust, be unevenly sharpened'. Don't fret. Our old friend the late Reverend G. A. Grace, one of the top ornamental turners and mechanics of his, or any other day, both formulated and solved this very problem. He made and set up a 12in (300mm) wheel with a perpendicular chuck for the cones. It was rotated by hand – a good swing and a light touch of the tool accurately on the dressed cone. He swung the wheel clockwise first, and then anti-clockwise and Gracefully, as in all his wonderful work, the tools were sharpened as well as they could possibly be.

Ornamental drills

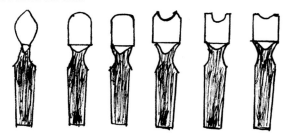

About a gross of drills were made for each instrument – a goodly number of shapes in graduated sizes. Should anyone elect to make drills, it's best to turn a number of blanks and then shape them as and when required. What do I do with my drill spindle? Well – not a tenth of what I could do, for the drill is an astonishing decorating tool.

MAKING CHESSPIECES
Often, in making chesspieces, I start my carving with the accurate drill, routing the slots and finishing the tops of the leaves with a thin, 2in (50mm) diameter carving cutter. Flutes or reeds, barleycorns, radial grooves, hemispheres known as pearls, all are accomplished by the drilling instrument. If I want a row of pearls around a box

I turn a bead with the very astragal drill I'll use to do

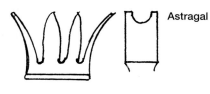
Astragal

Start carving with the accurate drill

the pearling in the drilling instrument.

You'll guess that there's a jig to hold each drill, not only for sharpening, but for use in the socket handle, into which it can be tightened with a thumbscrew. Thus, in this case, your drill can become a turning tool.

Drill holder and socket handle

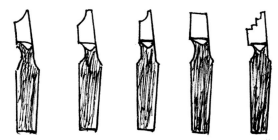

When the bead is turned, and made prominent by turning down a trifle on either side, the pearls are simply cut – but let me run through a little repetition job I had in January, in which the middle portions of chess tops and bases were made by a silversmith. These two-piece components all had to be alike.

Trumpet stem

Wood collet in two halves

The stem was a simple spindle-turned job drilled right through, with a male thread cut at the bottom end. To

43

chuck the turned stem I made a split collet in hardwood (about five minutes). I turned a piece of blackwood 1$\frac{5}{16}$in (33mm) in diameter, $\frac{11}{16}$in (18mm) wide, measured the diameter of the two parts of the stem where the collet would rest, and drilled an appropriate hole, slightly rounding the ends. I then sawed the collet in half and used it in the four jaw chuck.

For years I only had a three jaw chuck, and although I got the collets passably true with two jaws holding one half and one jaw the other, dead accuracy was rare. Now, with four jaws, it is fine. When you true the work in these, tap the wood collet, not the work. Believe it or not I used to tap the work, until a piece snapped. Blessed are those who do not have to pay for experience.

The tapping instrument is a ball pein hammer, 7oz (200g), with a long handle, 13in (330mm). The end of the handle rests on your right bottom rib and slides along the tool rest to tap the collet exactly where you want it.

But the trumpet end is the one we're focusing on now, not the stem. Cut the blank, prepare it for the three or four jaw chuck, face it nicely, and bore and cut an inside thread to fit a brass adapter chuck. These chucks are a great asset, and therein lies the advantage of thread chasing, because you can make any number of different adapters. If I couldn't chase threads I would use taps and dies – and I often do anyway.

Each one of the trumpets screws firmly on the adapter chuck, and I turn all as near alike as makes no difference. I use the very astragal drill in its jig and socket handle to form a bead at the end, finishing it nicely with a Holtz right quarter round tool in a socket handle. I then bore, cut an inside thread with chaser and armrest, and fit a stem firmly home.

When all are done, I polish on the calico buff with Cannings Crown compo. For ornamental turning, abrasives are never used on the parts that are to be decorated because the tools impart their own polished finish. Essentially, they must be 'got up' (as G.A. Grace used to insist) to sparkling sharpness. The edge would quickly deteriorate on a sanded surface.

CUTTING PEARLS

Now I can set up the slide rest with the drilling instrument clamped in it and the little astragal – specially sharpened – tightened in its socket. Carefully advancing the tool to its perfect engagement over the bead (using the lead screw, screw guide and depth stop), I set the index in the 144 hole and, after withdrawing the drill and setting the overhead in motion, I cut a tentative pearl using the operating handle and screw guide for perfect control.

If pearls are too close together they will cut into one another, if too widely spaced, columns will be left between them which will have to be removed. Under the magnifying glass I find nine pearls are too few, but 12, the next obtainable number, are too many. I need 10, which is every thirty-sixth hole in the 360 row. I might have marked them in white, but I didn't feel like fiddling with such close holes, so I decided to use the worm wheel and tangent (exciting ain't it?).

The wheel has 180 teeth, so fixing the tangent screw to engage the worm wheel, I removed the unnecessary index, turned the screw with the winch handle 18 times, and cut the next pearl – exactly right. To avoid wasting time I turned that handle pretty fast, once I'd gained confidence of course. For most pieces, at the conclusion of the 10 pearls, I'd find the index would still go into hole 144 – it was a means of checking. At the finish they were all, as near as makes no odds, a perfect likeness.

The drilling instrument is often the answer to certain jobs where accuracy is needed – getting perfect transverse holes for one – but in addition, you'll see many examples that display the wealth of beauty and variety that I wish I had time to emulate if you look through Holtzapffel Volume 5!

One of my greatest allies in this exacting work is my slant-lid mahogany box containing a gross or so each of slide rest tools, cutting frame tools and drills. Every one of the tools in that box, however tiny, can be used in socket handles, for hand turning (some with the aid of adapters). Without this shameless luxury, you must make more of your tools – you certainly can't buy 'em! You'd not only be broke, but infinitely worse off than the users of files.

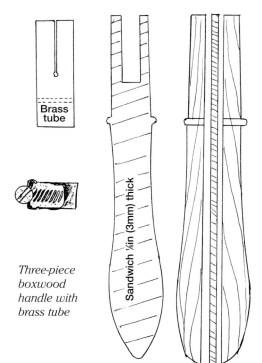

Three-piece boxwood handle with brass tube

For turners like me (I turn hardly anything bigger than a peppermill), you can't whack them. A handful of assorted three square files costs very little if you keep your eyes open, and you can quickly grind them to whatever shapes you like. If one turns out duff, little is lost – you can always use it to trim a new buff. The Holtzapffel box of tools of myriad shapes and sizes really eases things along, but don't cry if you haven't got one. You couldn't buy one for under four figures now anyway – and they encourage laziness!

The slide rest tools are about 3 x ¹¹⁄₃₂ x ⅛in (75 x 9 x 3½mm). Odd lengths this size can sometimes be found, or tools made up from old files, for use in the splendid socket handles which, I fear, hardly turn up at all now. If they did, someone would bid up to £50 – no joke. They are certainly cheaper to make than to buy. I make mine with three pieces of boxwood, two halves with a ⅛in (3½mm) leaf sandwiched between them. A section 1⅛ x ¹¹⁄₃₂in (30 x 9mm) is cut out of the business end of the leaf to accommodate the tool. Glue it all together

firmly, and turn the handle to the shape shown left – or any other shape if you prefer.

The top 2in (50mm) must fit tightly into a piece of brass or copper tube, about ⅝–¾in (15–18mm) in diameter, which is riveted right through where the dotted lines are. I also put a screw through the meaty part of the handle, but I inset the head leaving room for an ivory inlay to make it pretty. Polish on the buff of course.

With a ³⁄₁₆in (5mm) drill, bore right through the tube in line with the slot, then hacksaw down to the hole through the middle of the slot. If your leaf was the exact thickness of the tool steel, the tools will slide home perfectly, and can be tightened with a Jubilee clip from the ironmongers, trimming off the surplus tongue to neaten it.

I know you'll enjoy making a few of these – I recommend six at least. The actual tools you'll make can be decided according to requirements and need not be the same as those in the Holtzapffel boxes: you hardly make tools just to admire, make as many or as few as you need. I speak as one who is always busy. Were it not so, I can think of many worse things than devoting a few hours to making up tools you know will be useful ere long.

On re-reading earlier remarks, let no-one imagine there is any disgrace in turning out kitsch. It is, initially at least, practically unavoidable, and long may we enjoy it. If we have the courage to put the hammer on the worst of it, that might be a good idea too, but better to make kitsch than nothing – always remember, one man's kitsch is another man's masterpiece. Or, as Bertram replied to criticism, 'Someone will like it!'

Chapter 8
Ornamental Turning
ATTACHMENTS

I n Chapter 6, I made reference to the bridle, the purpose of which is to confine the head of the right hand guide screw, enabling the head of the tool to be advanced and withdrawn by winch-handle or key when only one hand is available. The operating lever cannot, of course, be used with bridle in position.

LIMITATIONS OF ORNAMENTAL SLIDE REST

The unaided ornamental slide rest can produce straight surface areas whether cylinder, cone or other shape. With the various cutting frames, a wide range of shapes can be contrived, providing a variety of work that would satisfy many turners. However, curves and shapes must

Above Holtzapffel rose cutting frame

Bridle and operating lever

be considered, and some ornamental turners do not turn by hand at all. If, for example, flutes, reeds and spirals are to follow a curved outline, an attachment known as the curvilinear apparatus is used. The photo, below, shows the simple apparatus in position – a stout bar running the whole length of the main slide, with a series of equi-distant, tapped holes to accommodate a template of steel, brass, or even Perspex, and elongated holes for adjustment, which can be fixed with two screws.

The curvilinear apparatus

In addition to the two clamping screws which secure the cutting frame or drilling instrument in the tool receptacle, an extra item is placed within the grooves in front of the rear clamping screw. Known as a rubber, it follows the curves of the template, ensuring that the tool exactly repeats the curves in both turning and decoration.

The rubber is quite prominent in the photo above, as are the two small countersunk screws which secure the bridle (now absent) to the right hand chamfer bar alongside the tool receptacle. As in hand turning, cuts are taken from the largest diameters downwards to avoid upsetting the fibres, which hate being rubbed up the wrong way.

Rubber

Now, if the bridle is in place, the tool cannot follow the template, so the bridle is removed (carefully replacing the screws which otherwise would get themselves lost!). The rubber is kept exactly following the template by use of the operating lever. Here I must say that a strong spring can be used in place of the operating lever – the ingenuity of some ornamental turners is never quite satisfied.

For years I had assumed that the operating handle was exclusively for curvilinear turning and I always – in common with most ornamental turners I know – used the bridle and winch handle (or key) to advance and withdraw the tool.

I tried the lever once (without the bridle of course), but found I couldn't control it with any delicacy. You cannot push a whirling fly-cutter in to cut freehand without dire risk of damage. After that I seldom removed the bridle, and I have happily used a key to operate the tool receptacle all these long and dusty years.

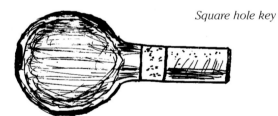

Square hole key

On one occasion, as I delicately wound the eccentric cutter the crucial last few thou onto the work, the cutter juddered home with resultant slight spoliation of the work. I concentrated with extra care for several more judders before it occurred to me to oil the slides of the tool receptacle, whereupon the improvement was laughably apparent. Don't let me catch any of you forgetting to oil the important little places regularly!

UNBRIDLED GUIDE SCREWS

Now, the answer lies in using the operating lever, but not freehand. I learned that the tool should be advanced by lever, but under the control of the unbridled guide screw: thus you have all the advantage of advancing the tool by hand lever, controlled by the guide screw with the other hand (without fear of judders) and whipping the tool back out of the way, instantly if necessary – it isn't always, I may say.

In practice, I keep a very firm, steady pull on the lever so that the guide screw is always pressing on the stop, and advance and withdraw the tool by turning the key or winch handle with the right hand.

> # NO longer may 'inferior' materials be denigrated as unworthy for ornamental turning: it's the workmanship that counts

Many do not use the operating lever, but let me quote from Holtzapffel Volume 5, 'The tool pressed forward by the lever, its gentle advance to penetrate the work and its quicker retreat from it, always regulated and controlled by the guide screw turned by the winch handle (or key)'. The pros and cons are described thus:

'The collar (or bridle) is removable and attaches by its base to the side of one of the chamfer bars of the cross slide above; it terminates in a fork that embraces the shaft of the guide screw and thus encloses the micrometer head of the latter between it and the upright post against which the head abuts.

'The lever, being for the time discarded, the tool is advanced and withdrawn from the work by gently turning the guide screw (the left

hand depth screw determining the depth of penetration). The bridle is an addition of great service and it would at first appear desirable that it should be used at all times instead of the lever, but there are several practical reasons that prevent its invariable employment which nearly confine its application to those numerous cases where one hand has to be otherwise engaged.

'The more immediate action of the lever is also frequently preferable, thus, so soon as the tool is disengaged from the material by a few turns of the guide screw, it may then be instantly thrown back by the lever to a more considerable distance from the work for examination of that or the tool, or for any other purpose, while with the bridle such withdrawal has to be effected by very many revolutions of the guide screw.

'The bridle cannot be used with the curvilinear apparatus. A stronger inducement to the use of the lever is that the cutting is usually found to be of rather better quality than when made under the control of the bridle, a circumstance doubtless due to the unfelt, but large and nearly perfect absorption of vibration into the elastic arm and frame of the operator caused by the pull of the hand on the lever.'

LEVER VERSUS BRIDLE

When I first learned all this, an opportunity to test the superiority of lever over bridle occurred almost at once. It was necessary to cut some pearls (hemispheres) with an astragal drill on African blackwood. Hitherto I have found that I cannot produce a perfect row as I do, sans bother, upon ivory; one or two pearls will crumble under the onslaught due to the jerkiness of the tool advance – however apparently infinitesimal. But with the lever, the advance is so controlled that, providing the tool is good and sharp, no failure is likely.

Of course, having never used the lever control before, I had to get accustomed to it, so the old saw applies, viz 'watch the quality – speed will come later'. I tried the ivory first and that is the one I made a muck-up of! When I got to the blackwood I had got used to it and all went perfectly.

African blackwood is really the best material, next to ivory, for ornamental turners because of its rare ability to receive a polished finish from the cutting tools whatever the direction of the grain. Now our ivory supplies are limited to whatever old stuff comes our way – and that for our own personal enjoyment – the rules of the game have changed as far as I'm concerned.

No longer may 'inferior' materials be denigrated as unworthy for ornamental turning: it's the workmanship that counts. Whenever I have ventured to try some woods which are really too soft, I have been entirely satisfied with the results, especially when the finish is assisted with the aid of a good wax polish and soft toothbrush.

VERTICAL CUTTING FRAMES

Let us consider next the vertical cutting frame (VCF) in which the tool, clamped in a mortise in the spindle, revolves in a vertical plane and removes segments of circles; it is capable of a wide variety of work.

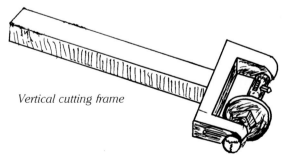

Vertical cutting frame

A round nose tool, traversed as it rotates, will cut broad flutes along a stationary cylinder or surface. Any number of pleasing shapes and many-sided figures can be cut on boxes, napkin rings or what you will, with the use of tools broad and narrow, and of a wide variety

of shapes, by making a series of segmental cuts, using the division plate and index in a continuous, intermediate or varying sequence of settings on each successive circle of cuts in close or wide juxtaposition. Who could put a limit on the variety of designs obtainable by emulation or experiment?

This type of VCF is considered best for wear and tear, but when the cuts have to be made close against the chuck, the width of the frame prevents its use. The VCF shown in the photo below (the lower tool) can, however, be used close to the chuck and is more convenient.

Eccentric cutting frame (top) and vertical cutting frame (bottom)

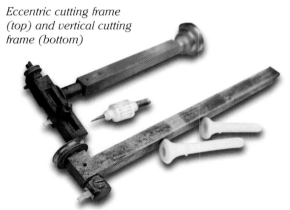

It is reputed to be subject to wear in the bearing, but having used this one for 30 odd years, keeping it (and one or two other things) well oiled, I cannot find the slightest evidence of wear and in fact, I do not now possess the other type at all. Further, I use a spliced rope overhead belt, which would mean unshipping the spindle to get the belt on the pulley of the other type – a chore to be avoided if possible.

ECCENTRIC CUTTING FRAMES

Perhaps the most enjoyable tool of all is the eccentric cutting frame (ECF), the upper tool in the photo above. It is also an exciting instrument for shaping, ornamenting and engraving. The square shank houses the revolving spindle, which carries a two-step pulley at the rear end.

At the front, set at right angles, is what might be termed a miniature slide rest. The tiny tool receptacle can be moved to any position along the slide, by turning its mainscrew. The receptacle is fixed at the required position by a square-headed screw which also clamps the tool.

If a point tool is set at zero, the centre will lie in the axial line of the spindle and a small dot can be cut, deepening into a conical hollow with increased penetration. The ECF is not eccentric at all in fact, but can be moved to and used in any eccentric position by the ornamental turning slide rest.

Tools with variously shaped edges will produce holes corresponding to those shapes. When the tool is moved to any other position on the slide, it cuts a circle the radius of which is the distance from the point of the tool to the axis of the spindle.

Quarter hollow tool The face of the slide upon which the small tool is clamped is diametrical, and therefore, the face of the tool, i.e. the cutting side, must lie upon it. In certain cases – where the frame is not in the way – the ECF can be used in place of the drilling instrument, for example, very large beads could be cut with a quarter hollow tool.

For cutting patterns of interlacing circles around a turned surface, the division plate and index is used in any required sequence of settings.

The mainscrew of the ornamental slide rest is used to give the adjustment of cuts when the pattern is required diametrically across the surface. Radical patterns can be made when the division plate and slide rest mainscrew are used.

By traversing the revolving tool along the work, broad or narrow recesses or flutes are cut, with sides matching the shapes of the tools used. Attractive stepped flutes are possible when the tool is adjusted to a smaller radius at each depth of cut. By traversing a round nose

tool, fixed at a wide radius, along a cylinder set by division plate and index to the appropriate four holes, square turning is easy.

A perfect hemisphere can be obtained by fixing the slide rest at an angle of 45° to the axis of a turned cylinder and, by trial and error, adjusting the tool radius and position until it touches the centre of the surface and the outside of the cylinder. The work would have to be turned roughly to shape before using the ECF, which would then be progressively advanced through several slow revolutions of the mandrel, by hand.

Prismatic, polygonal and all forms of geometric solids are within the scope of this master shaping and engraving tool; the more often it is used, the more will its manifold possibilities be revealed.

On some ECFs the head unscrews enabling other components, such as tiny drill chucks etc., to be used. Mine has that facility and I use it to great advantage.

For some reason this is frowned upon. Why? I quote: ' . . . the wear upon the fittings of the changeable parts and other incidental circumstances rapidly deteriorated the truth of revolution so necessary to the perfect working of the drills.' Oh yeah? Well it hasn't done so on mine in 30 years!

DON'T let me catch any of you forgetting to oil the important little places regularly!

The big ECF drawback is the out-of-balance displacement of weight at high speeds, as this causes unpleasant vibration. I have overcome this by using a balance weight, seen in the photos above right, fitted to the head. To be sure, it means drilling and tapping two 6BA holes in the slide – first removing the long lead

Balancing device, top side

Balancing device, underside

screw which could be damaged in the drilling.

As shown in the illustration below, it is simply a piece of mild steel or brass plate, bored to fit the end of the spindle against the cutter head, to which it is secured by two ³⁄₁₆in (5mm) x 6BA screws. Both plate and weight are slotted to allow adjustment and a little experiment will show its efficiency in obviating vibration, with the tool at any radius.

By far my best vibration obviator is the variable speed set-up shown in my Vampire lathe (see page 33 in Chapter 5). To be able to control the speed from zero to maximum by foot control is marvellous! As you advance the tool and cutting commences, there is always a

certain speed which achieves the finest result, and this you can control to great advantage. Of equal advantage is the ability to stop between cuts, at every adjustment of the index. This gives great assurance, as the cutter is whirring within a foot of your nose! Also, it's a saving of wear on the bearings.

There must be many thousands of turners who sigh enviously at the obviously tremendous advantages of variable speed for lathe and overhead. Fortunately, they now have the opportunity to join the enlightened, with negligible outlay, which may be the biggest advantage of all. If anything fails, you can set it right yourself, with no financial crisis.

*Construction of the
balancing device*

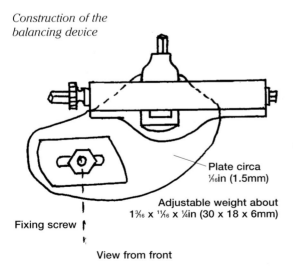

Fixing screw

Plate circa
¹⁄₁₆in (1.5mm)

Adjustable weight about
1³⁄₁₆ x ¹¹⁄₁₆ x ¼in (30 x 18 x 6mm)

View from front

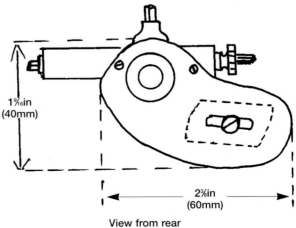

1⁹⁄₁₆in
(40mm)

2³⁄₈in
(60mm)

View from rear

Chapter 9
Decorative PATTERNS

The autumn leaves are heaped around the old shop door, clusters of umber, orange, red and gold that I enjoy and am in no hurry to clear away. Hawthorn branches over the skylight have piled leaves upon them. I must trim those branches later on. Not yet because they are full of red berries the blackbirds like and 'twould be wasteful.

There is a haven in the turning shop that is found in few other places, not that it is appreciated by many, otherwise there'd be more turners. I note the case of a blacksmith with a healthy business in a lovely village. His work was pleasurably varied, giving scope for many exciting engineering skills. He had the joy of being one of the most useful men and consequently popular for miles around.

Yet of six sons, not one elected to stay and take over from father: one and all left to join the factory environment in big towns. It seems to me they sold their freedom because, whereas the master craftsman greets the new day after the weekend with, 'Ah! Good old Monday!', and looks forward to his working week, your factory slave has the Monday blues, and well he might. Foolish indeed the one who throws aside such a wonderful opportunity to dance after the sickly pipe of Mammon. Few indeed get any choice in the matter, so I count myself one o' the blessed!

I often think of Britain's greatest turner, Joseph Mallord William Turner 1775–1851, misunderstood and maligned as a miser, yet a lovable man who retained nearly all his work to give to the nation. The nation was unworthy of him of course: 20,000 watercolours and 300 oils together with money to set them in a gallery, and few of the paintings were ever seen until comparatively recently.

His dear old father, a barber, called him Billy, and that's how I picture him, old Billy, who sat fishing at Petworth whenever he got the chance. But mostly he painted and 'tis said he accomplished more solid work in his lifetime than would make the lives of three ordinary artists.

Think of the occasion when he had one of his best paintings hung in the Royal Academy. It completely eclipsed a smaller picture next to it, a fine painting by a little-known artist who anxiously expected to be hopelessly outshone by that adjacent brilliance. It was so unfortunate that this occasion, so vital to him, should have turned out so strategically disastrous due to the luck of the draw and the hanging committee.

Left *Alternative ivory, hand-screwed ornamental box, 3in (75mm) in diameter*

On varnishing day, before the public exhibition, when the exhibitors were permitted to touch up their pictures, Billy was there and do you know what he did? He deliberately painted a dull wash over his mouthwateringly blue sky!

'Why man!', exclaimed a friend, 'you have ruined your picture!'

'No, no!' said Billy, 'it will wash off afterwards,' (it was an oil painting) 'and it will give the other fellow a vastly better showing!'

What a story – and what a wonderful man! We can't all be brilliant – what a bore if we all were – but we can be considerate and kind and give others a sporting chance. So many look for perfection and sometimes they think they can see it. Some are so hooked on this will-o'-the-wisp they deem their own work 'far too 'umble' to put on the show table, yet those who exhibit know – none better – that their work is often far from perfect. You get fed up with perfectionists!

CLEVER DICKS

A cockney pal of mine exemplified this when I showed him a box I'd just made; 'Cor! I 'ate clever dicks!' I'll tell you about that box.

I had a selection of work on show at Apothecaries Hall on a Worshipful Company

The two ornate ivory boxes I bought years ago, which introduced me to ornamental turning and inspired this project

of Turners, and their ladies, day. The items that attracted the most attention from the ladies were a couple of ornate screwed boxes which weren't even my work. They were a couple I bought years ago, when ornamental turning and I hadn't been introduced.

I decided to make a couple about 1¾ x 2in (45 x 50mm), with some basketwork made with the vertical cutting frame, and tops decorated with the eccentric cutting frame. They were hand-turned in my usual way.

Start by securing the cylinder (be it ivory, blackwood, polyester or whatever you can lay your hands on!) in the three jaw, self-centring chuck. Turn the surface and face, then hollow the lid to pre-determined depth, using your armrest of course.

DRAWING

It is always best, I find, to make a simple drawing on squared paper in order to ensure getting the proportions right, as I did in the illustration below, rather than playing it by ear as you go along. You may get away with it

Basketwork pattern design

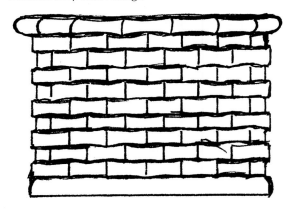

without the aid of a drawing – I'm sure you will – yet frequently it's a great help in saving time and material. Further, your book of squared paper will gradually fill up with sketches and projects which will always be a source of ideas for future work and repeat orders.

If you draw as you work out the best ways of

carrying out the projects, don't forget to make notes of any methods, measurements and details which had to be thought out carefully, because it's not unknown to get asked for one of the same, long after you've forgotten everything! Then your joy as you unearth those valued details will make your day! If I hadn't made notes and sketches I should never have enjoyed sharing them with others.

Of course, you'll say you can't draw, but everyone can – if they want to: to draw a symmetrical figure simply draw one side of the profile, fold the drawing down the middle and cut round it with scissors. When opened out and laid on the page, it is simple to pencil all round it, then finish it beautifully in ink. Actually, one side of the profile with measurements is sufficient, but I prefer to see the whole, as it avoids that 'something missing' feeling.

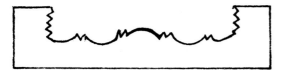

The basketwork pattern cut inside the box lid

I cut an inside thread with armrest and size 20 chaser, then make a pattern inside the lid, shown above, with flat point and round nose tools. Not at all necessary this, but polished nicely it looks rather well. If it's ivory, billiard balls, etc., Brasso on cotton wool imparts a lustre nothing can beat.

Cut the lid off. Cut the matching outside thread on the body of the box, taking great care, until the lid fits truly. My variable speed foot control makes this far less difficult, as I can come down to 100rpm, but when I recently had to manage on an ordinary lathe, I found the fixed slow speed of 400rpm no great drawback. I've always said you can get used to anything!

To help screws catch with facility, I make the tiniest hollow at the beginning of the screw with a ⅛in (3mm) round nose tool, after the fit

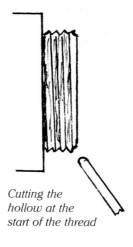

Cutting the hollow at the start of the thread

has been perfected. It can be embarrassing when someone takes five seconds before they succeed in what should be the simple operation of screwing on a box lid. The screw fit should not be slack, as it will be easier when polished. Hollow the interior to your liking and polish.

The lid is then screwed home fairly tightly. This is to have 16 scallops around the top using an astragal tool in the vertical cutting frame, but to make less work for the tool, plain turn the bead first, using the same tool clamped in a receptacle, which in turn is clamped into the socket handle. I then turn three concentric v-cuts on the surface, with a flat point tool. At this point, the

The astragal tool

surface of the lid is fully polished on the calico buff with Cannings Crown compo. Abrasives are never used on work on which ornamental tools are to be used because it can be harmful to the delicate, polished edges of the tools.

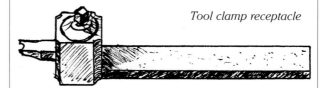

Tool clamp receptacle

The astragal tool is fixed in the vertical cutting frame after first sharpening on a revolving brass cone smeared lightly with fine grinding paste, and finishing by rubbing the face on Arkansas stone.

I do most of my plain turning on the Acorn capstan headstock (with Timken taper-roller

Socket handle

bearings) which for me is always a delight to use. To decorate the box, I remove it from the chuck on the Acorn, and fix it dead true in the three jaw on my Holtz Eldorado. This has the same variable speed overhead gear as my Vampire except that the standards were cast (to the pattern initiated by Evans) in light alloy and painted battleship grey.

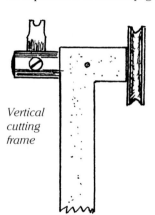

Vertical cutting frame

One good thing about ornamental turning is that it cannot be rushed and it absorbs your whole attention. The vertical cutting frame is clamped in the tool receptacle and the slide rest is adjusted so the tool has sufficient clearance and not too much overhang, which might create the possibility of vibration.

Revolving brass cone for sharpening

Everything is common sense really, but if you're in a hurry it's possible to forget to tighten the slide rest clamping screw below the lathe bearers! And don't let anyone tell you you won't make the same mistake twice – or more!

SHAVINGS

The driving belt can be arranged over the pulleys to run clockwise or anti-clockwise. Do you want the fly-cutter to revolve upwards so that the shavings may get in your eyes? Or down so that the pressure on the lid under the onslaught unscrews it with deleterious results?

With specs on, I disregard shavings and vote for the upward cutting.

We want the scallops to just meet, barely reducing the diameter. To make sure, a pencil line around the periphery will reveal exactly when the right depth of cut has been reached. I choose every ninth hole on the 144 row to achieve 16 scallops. With the aid of the depth stop I obliterate the pencil mark between the first two cuts, then complete the rest. Of course, when the precise depth of penetration has been found, a square-headed screw is tightened to clamp the depth stop safely.

Having completed the scallops, I exchanged the astragal for a flat tool, ⅛in (3mm) wide, and began to put some basketwork on the lid and body.

Now, had I made it 18 segmental cuts per row, I could have used every eighth hole in the 144 circle, and for the next adjacent row to be exactly midway, simply begun on the fourth hole instead of the first. However, I cut 16 again so that, in order to get the next row midway, I had to change from the ninth hole to the fourth hole, and make up the difference by adjusting the screw on the index. Of course, the perfectionist would never make such a mistake and if faced with such a problem he'd take the time to make mathematical adjustments. The lesson is to note these errors and try to remember not to do it again.

After a couple of rows I found the flat cuts were very poor and I couldn't get that tool to cut well. I tried a file on it and it was soft! No wonder the cuts were striated! I didn't change to a better tool because the whole design lacked any charm. I decided the appearance of the astragal cuts was so attractive, I'd continue on the body with a smaller astragal tool, taking it deep enough to obliterate the flats.

SCREW JOIN

I began where the screw join is, working first to the top, then going back to the join and working to the base, each circle of cuts exactly meeting the next, but midway. The last row before you come up to the top of the lid left a strip of no-man's-land about ¹⁄₁₆in (1.5mm), and the same at the bottom, but I find these things usually sort themselves out – that's half the fun, isn't it?

Next I exchanged the vertical cutting frame in the slide rest for an eccentric cutting frame, and adjusted the slide rest 90°, to face the surface of the lid which I now proposed to decorate.

I used a point tool, at about a 50° angle, sharpened accurately in the goneostat, and made a light pattern of cuts after the style shown below, which is merely a guide and doesn't have to be followed.

Point tool for decorating the lid

Lid decoration pattern

By trial and error you can simply enjoy trying out any patterns without limitations. Usually they'll look quite impressive, and they can be done on any odd discs, ad infinitum. Of course, any that take your fancy can be noted down in detail for repetition.

COCK-UP

Okay, let's see what sort of master cock-up I have made! I take it out of the chuck for finishing in the Acorn. A little narrow tool clears the excess left below the rim of the lid. With lid removed, I check the bottom by opening the jaws of the chuck inside. Care, experience and a light touch enable you to handle work of this sort in the three jaw, but it could have been pressed on a wood plug gripped in the chuck

more safely. I turned the base and put a little plain moulding where necessary.

The mating surfaces of the screw fitting had been impaired a trifle and a slight hair parting appeared on one side, as I'd had to remove a bit more material by obliterating the flat cuts. Then I got busy on the most important work – the finish on the buff. I always go contra to all the ornamental turning pundits by buffing some – not all – of my ornamental work. When – or if – you see work that has been spoiled by the buff you'll know it's not mine; I'd put the hammer on it first!

The box was quite attractive, although imperfect, and I sold the mate to it (which I made at the same time) to one of the ladies and got an unsolicited testimonial. I hung on to the other for as long as I could, but eventually someone insisted on buying it.

There is a lesson to be learned and it's this: never cut into the mating surfaces of a screwed box with segmented cuts when ornamenting, as the fit can be disturbed. I have seen the lid tighten a trifle as the fly-cutter cuts into the join. It is better to turn plain beads where the join is, and do the ornamenting above and below.

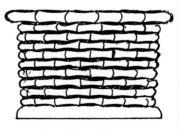

The finished box

Two final points. Polishing is a very personal matter. The late G. H. Grace – famous ornamental turner – eschewed the buff, but all his splendid work was impeccably lustrous. He liked Brasso though.

And back to drawing: it helps turning enormously, but your work seldom, if ever, finishes up exactly like the drawing because the hand and eye of a good turner usually improve on the illustration and fashion the ideal design as the work progresses. That's my excuse anyway!

Chapter 10 ● *Restoring* CHESSPIECES

*B*e adventurous where materials are concerned! When I turn harder materials, the square tool is used in place of the skew and, quite often, a round nose instead of a gouge. When I describe my work in ivory, I'm referring to my trade, which goes back to biblical times, and although ivory has been supplanted by plastics and other things, there is plenty of old stuff around for restoration, for which I have developed a useful knack of finding just what is needed out of my bits and pieces store. This is no big deal because my working hours have dwindled down to a precious few. Therefore, when I describe ivory turning, the material could as well be boxwood, blackwood or bone, and the time period any time within the last 20 years. After which preamble I will begin.

Are you surprised when I say I'm going to make a Jaques' pawn? I surprise myself! It's happened after half a century, that I have discovered I'm an artist. I had a set of Jaques Staunton chesspieces to restore, with lots of chipped collars and bases. They were rather too thin and could hardly be expected to survive, bouncing about unprotected in their box for more than a century. They just weren't valued. But three pawns were slightly different.

The ivory was soft – not the hard Congo of the Jaques. The balls were a shade bigger and the stems screwed into the bases flat instead of countersunk, which is an inviolable feature of all Jaques' chesspieces. Then the actual shape of the balls impinged on the little grey cells – also the beautifully cut screws – and I knew Bertram had restored this set many years ago.

For some time I used a steel tube to get the balls perfect, but, you know, once perfection is in your eye you can, and should, eschew that tube. I see three types of pawn spheres; Jaques', Bertram's, and my own. None are absolutely perfect, so they are individually recognizable – and as you know, nothing is so boring as perfection.

NOTHING is so boring as perfection

So, how does this make me an artist? Well, it's the heart really. Bertram wouldn't have bothered to notice the trifling differences: I did and I replaced all three with matching ivory turned to be indistinguishable from the Jaques' pawns. I simply wouldn't have been happy if I didn't accept the challenge.

Left *Polyester resin Copenhagen king, 6in (150mm), made in 12 separate pieces*

MAKING A PAWN

To make a pawn:

1 Cut and prepare stem and base, which includes hubbing ends circular.
2 Fix the stem in a three jaw by one end, and carefully turn ⁷⁄₁₆in (12mm) cylindrical – and surface cleanly. Measure and mark the exact length to where the screw begins.
3 Reverse in the chuck and turn the screw with countersink and correct diameter.

Thread cut on the pawn stem

4 Polish the threads on buff (only a fool of an artist would do that, but it makes a better fit).
5 Fix the base in the three jaw, turn a countersunk thread to fit the stem, either with chaser or tap (preferably both), and tighten the stem with pliers permanently. If the stem is not running true enough, tap it true with a small hammer on the base (not the stem) after loosening the chuck a trifle.
6 Turn the end down to ball diameter plus ¹⁄₃₂in (1mm), then with a vernier calliper (or your favourite weapon) set to the diameter of the ball, marking with a pencil where the middle of the ball will come. Turn the ball, but not to finished exactitude.

Middle of the ball marked with a pencil line

7 I never measure the distance to the collar – it comes just where it will after turning the best sphere that I can. Pencil a dot on the front end of the ball before you come round with a square tool on the armrest. It's easy to leave a flat at the top, but not

when you turn the pencil dot out. Follow the arrow round with a ¹⁄₁₆in (1.5mm) round nose tool on the armrest – to me it's as efficacious as a mahl-stick. Get a good hemisphere at the front first, but do not obliterate the pencil line half way.

8 Turn the back half with a right oblique tool.
9 Now complete the sphere to its right diameter, and turn the collar with a left oblique tool.

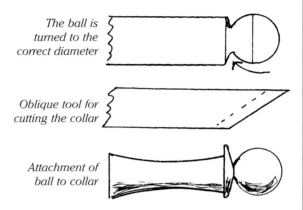

The ball is turned to the correct diameter

Oblique tool for cutting the collar

Attachment of ball to collar

FOR BEST RESULTS

It's a tricky job to get your perfect ball attached to the collar with just the right diameter in the join (can't call it a neck because there is no neck). The diameter where it meets the collar is about ⅛in (3mm) – sets vary. Some chess makers prefer such fragility that pieces easily chip or break when dropped. It is easier to make such stuff than repair it.

The important thing is that all 16 pawns should be pretty well alike, but where people are over-critical I recommend moulded sets. If they haven't yet learned that it is the small discrepancies that constitute the essential charm of hand work, I can teach them nothing.

I remember Bertram being badgered by an unappreciative, pernickety client who returned a batch of work for a trifling fault. Bertram simply put it in a drawer and left it until asked for. When this occurred in a week or two he returned them untouched and of course, all was well.

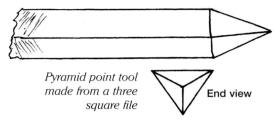

Pyramid point tool made from a three square file **End view**

To get the best result when turning the ball where it joins the collar, I use my point tool. Not the flat point but the triangular pyramid made from a three square file. The armrest is not needed with the point tool. Practice will prove its usefulness.

When making a whole set, hopefully the bases will be turned from prepared lengths of material, but for the odd repair I go to the bits and pieces department where I usually find just the discs I require. It may be the exact thickness with nothing for the chuck: it is then that the illustration below becomes clear.

The part in the self-centring chuck cannot be turned until last, but you can either grip the rounded part indicated by the arrow in the illustration below – lightly – and finish the base with an oblique tool, or unscrew the stem and screw the base on an adapter plug.

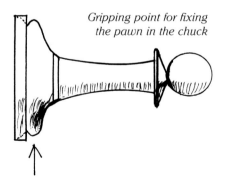

Gripping point for fixing the pawn in the chuck

Of course, all this work is an exercise in lightness of touch. If you hold finished pieces in a self-centring chuck so as not to bruise the material, you must apply the lightest of pressure on good sharp tools.

It reminds me of the ancient art of angling, where the highly skilled endeavoured to land roach up to a pound on a single horse hair. All

I got was a two ounce gudgeon. A safer method is to lap a strip of glasspaper around the part where the jaws grip. They may then be tightened a little more without bruising. You learn by experience.

INSPIRATION

Now that pawn is a tricky little job to get perfect, yet it cannot be called complex by any stretch of the imagination. So why do I detail it so carefully? Well, I was thinking, and looking at some of the complex work described in books and photographs. I wondered how many readers would be capable of imitating it. Hardly one in a hundred. So why bother to instruct the vast majority who will never – or hardly ever – make any attempt to do so, although I know very well that many could aspire to such work?

I'll tell you what it is by giving an illustration from the arts. Why do people like me buy books of encouragement and instruction by fine watercolourists and the like when we know we may never paint like the authors? The reason is simply that we enjoy the pictures and descriptions of the methods. We are inspired by them and venture to hope that some of the genius may one day rub off on us. The fact that it seldom does is of not the slightest importance and doesn't spoil our enjoyment. The only way is to do plenty of simple work instead of always attempting some impossible masterpiece.

I can affirm that one who habitually works on simple things will become capable of greater things, but beginners attempting it in the reverse order may well give up in despair. When I left school I worked for five years on the very simple trivia of hand turnery and had very little confidence that I could tackle better work. Yet, when the time came and I was thrown in the deep end, I discovered I had nearly all the skills needed. The only thing lacking was brains, but even that is relatively unimportant when we can pick others' brains at will. And that is why I have described the simple, but beautiful pawn.

Finally, on this simple theme, it is maddeningly true that even simple things require skill that can be acquired only by unremitting practice.

TURNING IVORY

January 1. It's New Year's Day, how quiet! As usual I make time to visit my best friends, my lathes. Music from Vienna is on Radio 3 and with Mozart and Strauss, what better company could be asked?

I'm making eight pawns to complete a beautifully delicate old ivory set by Calvert. I have plenty of work to fill up the time I have to spare – which isn't as much as I'd like – and being an old ivory turner I have a modest store of old ivory. Indeed some, being mammoth, goes back to the flood, so I defy anyone to accuse me of contributing to the extinction of the mammoth, by thunder!

I had cut and hubbed the pieces ready for the chuck and they'd been soaking in water for a day, which makes them delightful to turn. If you find the grain tends to pick up when ivory has been soaked, remember, nothing is ever perfect, and softer ivory is preferable to brittle, especially if your finishing cuts are made very lightly and with keen tools. Further, the grain in dry, brittle ivory can also pick up if badly turned. Do not soak too long though – say half a day or so.

CHUCKING METHODS

Now, these long, slender turnings can be turned between centres, but then comes the problem of chucking them to complete the

front end. Not too difficult, but if we can turn them in one, we should.

I always used to drive them into an iron chuck in days before 'bone grubbers' got spoiled with luxuries like self-centring chucks, but for these pawns I use the four jaw, geared scroll, self-centring chuck – an unashamed, super-duper addition to the three jaw.

The old bone turners – and I started as such back in '33 – used a short-handled 1½lb (680g) hammer to drive long pieces of prepared bone into an iron chuck with slightly tapered hole, after chalking the end to aid grip.

As the bone was held all the way round, it nearly always stayed put depending on several things:

1 that it had been hubbed to a good fit in the chuck, i.e. circular and slightly tapered;
2 that it had been well rubbed on the ball of whitening every turner kept on the bench;
3 that it had been firmly and carefully driven in; and
4 that tools were not allowed to catch or get blunt enough to require force which would fetch the bone out of the chuck.

Of course, it did come out now and then, when the challenge was to replace it without damage. Two out of three times we did.

When Bertram and I became lone turners after WWII he was in the Cotswolds and I in London, but we kept in touch by letters as he steered me along in my early days. I have a boxful of those letters, some of which are priceless!

We gave up bone, as that branch of the trade had dwindled to practically nothing. We

Turn long, slender pieces in one if possible

weren't sorry as it was hard work. For small jobs normally requiring bone we used ivory waste at no extra charge – and I still do.

I stopped using the iron chucks when much of the repetition work faded because it was easier to use a self-centring chuck than make extra chucks for odd sizes. If you use a three jaw, you first turn the end to be gripped parallel, and hold it in the chuck by at least ⅙in (4mm). You can tighten the jaws as firmly as you like – and it has to be firm or it will not hold for such long work. Bruising doesn't matter as it has to be made into a screw at that end.

IT is maddeningly true that even simple things require skill that can be acquired only by unremitting practice

The three jaw, of course, only grips in three places, and with soft ivory may fail if too much pressure is applied to the tools, but, if a four jaw chuck is used it adds so much to the gripping proclivities that you will be delighted.

I have found a couple of other advantages in the addition of a four jaw to my box o' tricks. It will centralize pieces which won't quite run true in the three jaw. By the same token, the three jaw will suit what the four jaw will not, and as I can change chucks and adjust the tool rest in 20 seconds flat it is not a whit inconvenient.

As the four jaw grips in four places, it saved one job which the three jaw was ruining. I was finishing some polyester organ stop bushes and, as I gripped them to round the tops and open to the required inside diameter, leaving quite a thin wall, nearly every one cracked because of too much space between the jaws. I substituted the four jaw and lo! all was right as right can be – with the extra support.

Further to our list of advantages. As you may

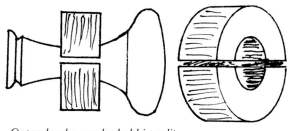

Organ knobs can be held in split boxwood collets

know, I use split boxwood collets to hold various things – especially organ draw-stop knobs, as can be seen above. I fix them in the three jaw so that two jaws grip half the collet, and the third jaw grips the other half. Then, by tapping the collet, not the draw-stop knob, with a tiny hammer, I get it as true as I can, but it is seldom truly accurate, though the error isn't observable on the finished knob. But now I use the four jaw and get an even grip all around, and feel thoroughly spoiled with such luxury.

Hand work is not precision engineering and is attended with many small – and occasionally glaring – inaccuracies which some eulogize over, making a virtue of necessity. But when you can improve accuracy I, for one, am pleased.

Indeed, it is only when you have experienced ornamental turning that something akin to perfection enters the mind. Until then the yardstick for measuring excellence is relatively poor. Once ornamental turning is experienced, never again will full satisfaction be gained from ordinary work, because the memory of excellence never fades. Really then, even though so much of my work is by hand, at heart it is all ornamental turning. (That is my story anyway.)

One more point about the four jaw – of course it's the most important! I was cutting short lengths off a rod of casein, supporting the free end with the right hand and parting off with the screever in my left – you have to be ambidextrous – when I carelessly allowed the screever to jerk forward at the end of its cut, precipitating part of my index finger against the chuck. The jaws were only exposed a trifle at the outer ends, but as I had (astoundingly) omitted to grind off the sharp corners, I received minor lacerations. How I came to leave that one chuck unmodified I cannot fathom, but 'tis well and truly done now. Procrastination does wonders for the Elastoplast trade!

SHARPENING

It's Monday morning again – a frosty one – and my Acorn lathe with Timken roller bearings takes a few minutes to warm up.

I clamp a chunk of soaked ivory in the three jaw. Not quite achieving the higher speed I wanted, the piece flew at the onslaught of my ⅜in (10mm), light turning gouge, impingeing on my finger painfully en passant. This is sheer carelessness and quite unnecessary, occasioned by impatience: I should have allowed for lack of speed by using lighter pressure, or waited until the lathe gathered speed, and I should have put a better edge on that gouge, but like so many, I work with dull tools a bit longer instead of doing what I must do now: sharpen!

I sharpen with a rocking movement on the medium India stone, finishing with a gouge slip and finally stabbing into the end grain of my rough timber bench in the time-honoured way, to remove any whiskers. All the old turners I knew did this, but of course they didn't aspire to

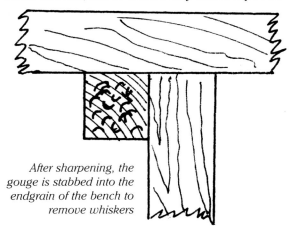

After sharpening, the gouge is stabbed into the endgrain of the bench to remove whiskers

A size 20 chaser is used to cut the grooves in the top ball

beautiful mahogany lathe beds.

Try again – what a difference! It cuts so well I seriously wonder why I allow any tool to get blunt at all. Only laziness I suppose. While I'm at it, I grind my point tool and chaser. The latter, a size 20, I use to make the grooves in the top ball. It is hollow ground, but barely touches the teeth, which are finished flat on the India stone. The grinding is only occasional.

COPYING PATTERNS

There are different ways of copying a pattern and you are not bound for life to only one. On this occasion I chuck the hubbed piece by the base and turn down the other end to a cylinder (slightly larger than the ball) for about ½in (12mm). Then I reverse to do the same with the base end, leaving it slightly larger in diameter and surfacing it cleanly. Next, I chuck this end by ⅛in (4mm), and that will hold.

I measure and turn the correct length and as the turning gets under way, every measurement is done with the one vernier calliper and pencil, always measuring twice. Here I must strongly urge you to have a calliper that clamps positively! I can't number the times I've had my work undersized due to a calliper slipping – and according to Murphy's law, they never slip the generous way! I find it more convenient to adjust the one calliper for each measurement, in length and diameter, than to set a number of measuring tools and then try to find them.

I don't adhere to this method if the number of measurements is few. In such cases I set the requisite callipers and dividers and hang them on a small tool stand to be selected and replaced in chronological order.

A CHALLENGE

Here's a curious chucking challenge I've just encountered that Sherlock Holmes might have called a 'three pipe problem'. A very fine old carved chess set had rooks in the form of elephants with castles on their backs. I don't think the castles were actually turned *in situ*, but they were near enough round and all made in the solid, the elephants being some 1¹⁵⁄₁₆in (50mm) long. The problem was that two had broken castellations which required turning off and replacing. How do you chuck an elephant and get the castle running true – and furthermore forsooth, with the customer waiting hopefully!

These elephant rooks posed a chucking challenge

In the tobacco pipe trade they use a hornbeam chuck with an appropriate section cut out with a bandsaw – or even bowsaw – to accommodate the pipe bowl while it is being bored. The split hole at the front is tightened onto the briar by driving a metal ring on the tapered front end.

I made a similar chuck years ago and have used it a couple of times in 40 years. The interior required a little more excavation to take the elephant, but the hole at the front was too large for the castles. I simply made a boxwood collet bored to the diameter of the castles, and slightly tapered to match them. The outside diameter was made to fit the chuck, and the collet sawn in two.

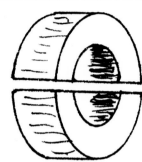

Boxwood collet for fitting in the chuck

The elephant was carefully manoeuvred into the chuck with the collet in position and the ring tapped on to tighten. The beauty of the arrangement is that this chuck has a solid end which is clamped in the four jaw chuck so that not only can the castle be trued in the chuck by tapping the collet – never the castle! – but the chuck can be tapped true in the four jaw.

The ensuing work, in this case cutting off the damaged ends and boring and cutting threads for the replacement tops, is, of course, done at a very low speed with keen tools. I call that 'The Master's Chuck'!

My client, who enjoyed the whole proceedings, rewarded what he called a miraculous job by upping my modest charge by 66⅔%.

A hornbeam chuck with a section cut out for boring a pipe

Chapter 11 ● *Design* INSPIRATION

ere I shall describe a project I made some years ago, in ivory. Other materials, including hardwoods, could, of course, be used, and I am sure it will prove of interest – maybe even to non-turners!

It was January 5. I went to St Martin's Court off the Shaftesbury Ave, to deliver some ornamental peppermills to my good friend Dennis Strange in his antiques and silverware shop. I'd been trying to design something superb in the sugar sifter line because it was by no means certain that sufficient support would be forthcoming for the special competition arranged for the Society of Ornamental Turners by the Worshipful Company of Turners who, of course, we didn't want to let down.

Now the ideas I sketched were definitely 'all right' and, as you know, anything that is all right is obviously all wrong for such a competition. An entry to be worthy of more than a glance needs something extra, unless one is simply intending to 'make the numbers up'.

Speaking professionally, I intended my pair either to win or to be readily saleable to one or other of my old friends, because the outlay of money and time is not something I've ever been wealthy enough to squander willy-nilly.

So, I'd more or less given up my own notions for the design as a bad job, and I put the problem to my friends in St Martin's Court, hoping they'd have an idea or two. They did! They showed me some silver samples from their catalogues that were exquisite. Then Dennis produced an eighteenth century silver sifter about 4½in (115mm) high, that had just been cleaned. Right away I could visualize my exact model, and over a sandwich and a pint of cider in the tavern next door, he offered to lend the sifter to me. Its value was £350.

At home, I scaled it up to 7in (180mm) high on squared paper, with the necessary modifications for the change of material from silver to ivory, and I could hardly wait to

Left *Ivory patterns for the Indian-style chess set, 7in (178mm)*

make the prototype. I made it up without the smallest difficulty – except for the problem of devising the pattern of the holes. It is the holes that can make or mar a sifter, castor or dredger of this kind.

When I'd finished it, it was passed as beautiful by all and sundry – including my sternest critic, my wife, Olive – and clearly needed no further embellishment.

A word about design and embellishment. The designer, looking for something original, can rest assured that whatever he comes up with, if it's any good at all, has been done, near enough, before. If it really is 100% original it will be hideous, which is why so much modern design is tasteless.

Indeed, when someone talks about modern design you know, before you see it, it's going to be bald, banal and boring like the modern office block, often because the better things of the past were made when materials were cheap and there were plenty of highly skilled craftsmen – also cheap.

So much of the sneering about richly ornate designs of the past – especially in architecture – is really sour grapes. How they'd love the opportunity to do so lavishly today! So they make a virtue of necessity and kid themselves it's good when anyone can see it is kitsch!

Personally I dislike labels like 'old fashioned' and 'modern'. While there is room for a wide variety of tastes and preferences, there is ugliness in both modern and old designs, but good taste and beauty have survived as long as man has, right up to the present day.

Never be shy of taking what you want from every source of inspiration and adapting to your own fancy – occasionally you may even (perhaps by accident) break out in genuine originality! We might even yet produce some designs in this century that future centuries might hold up as good!

When you have made your piece – with or without embellishment – don't feel obliged or

The design for the sugar sifters

in duty bound, just because you happen to possess a lot of ornamental turning apparatus, to overdo things. Know when to stop – which isn't always easy!

If you want to run riot with your ornamental turning gear, make it joyful and unashamed, and if folk choose to call it old fashioned, let them. You enjoyed making it and we will enjoy it too. As Ron Ranson said, 'If you're going to have a failure make it a glorious failure!' In the case of the sugar sifter competition there were several factors to be considered, and this design had to be tempered with restraint.

A Turner's Lament

How shall I replace you, dear gouge of old,
A faithful companion for many long years?
Your form is quite shrunken, your colleagues all sold
And for your successor I've very grave fears
He's long, proud & shining enough it is true,
Like many productions of this modern age,
But damnit! on cutting he hasn't a clue!
As edge crumbles off him I inwardly rage,
And take up my old friend, now two inches long,
Or short it'd be perhaps better to say
And soliloquise glumly, "We'll stick it, old son,
But they don't make a lot that's worth tuppence today!"

About a fortnight before the due date of the competition, I sorted out a piece of suitable material, but it was the final week before I began. I wrote down the details of making as I went along, and here they are.

ROUGH TURNING

In the days when ivory – and everything else – was cheap, stocks of such wide variety were available that no wastage occurred. It is well said that ivory never gets any less – the pieces simply get smaller. But now waste is not easy to avoid, and as the pair of sifters had to match, they had to come from the same piece.

The six sections for the sifters marked out on the ivory

I cut the six sections, pencilled circles of the correct diameter on the ends, and sawed them close. Then I hubbed the ends with my large cutter (you know my methods) for gripping in the three jaw chuck. I might have used cup chucks, but I find the three jaw more convenient – it's all a matter of personal preference, which varies with time and experience. No two turners work the same, and I have changed many things over the years.

If the piece to be gripped in the three jaw is almost the finished diameter, I protect it from bruising with a doubled piece of old glasspaper.

When rough turning large ivory you may use a ⅜in (10mm) gouge. Bertram normally did, and got through a goodly number in his lifetime. I wrote a bit of doggerel about a dear old gouge of mine 30 odd years ago. It was only about 2in (50mm) long, but of such good steel that I actually still have it for occasional use.

I usually reserve gouges for hardwood; for ivory I use a stout, three square file, ground to a round nose of about 3/16in (5mm) radius. Now, when your workpiece is very firmly chucked, you may safely take heavy cuts with your large round nose, but when your work is in the three jaw, it is vulnerable until turned smooth. The safest tool to use in roughing down cylinder or surface is a little round nose tool, ground from a small, three square file, tapped into a length of broomstick about 9in (230mm), and ferruled.

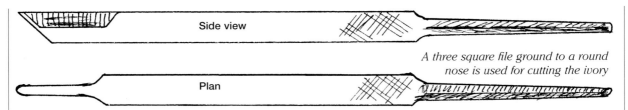

Side view

Plan

A three square file ground to a round nose is used for cutting the ivory

You may well decide to make real respectable handles, but a well-finished and buff-polished broomstick handle is perfect for me – for this tool and also long screevers. For the armrest I like a good, stouter boxwood handle.

This narrow tool in its extended handle, held at the end, does wonders in the cutting line, without sweat, and greatly reduces the risk of work flying out of the chuck to all but nil. Once the stuff is turned smooth, it is quite safe. Ooops! – well almost!

We have two bottoms to be turned and, as they're to be a pair (any fool can make one!), select the piece with the smaller diameter and keep it as large as it will yield – you can then make the second to match, whereas, if you start with the larger, you may find the second a bit too small – I know!

Chuck it by the base end, turn cylindrical and surface. Chuck by the top end and turn it reasonably near the required shape, leaving a little for finishing. If a hole has to be stopped in the bottom (tusks are hollow for one-third of their length), open, and cut an inside thread (30 or 32), making a countersunk edge.

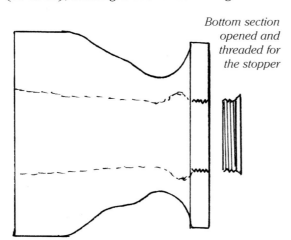

Bottom section opened and threaded for the stopper

With the small round tool, undercut the inside a little, leaving the threads about ⅛in (4mm) in depth – the thickness of the stopper. Turn the base almost down to the required diameter. Chuck by the base and turn the shape, taking your time and using a cardboard template to check as you go along. 'Never hurry now, for time's all sweet.'

The top bead is made, using the same bead tool you'll use in the vertical cutting frame later, to cut the scallops. You will not be able to complete the shape right up to the base at this stage, of course.

Now, open the inside, following fairly, but not fastidiously, the outside contour. Do not attempt to make it thin – leave that to those who enjoy that brand of wizardry. Cut a good inside thread – 20 teeth per inch for preference.

You will, of course, have determined all your measurements, inside and out, in advance. Finish the interior with glasspaper and Brasso on cotton wool, running the chaser into the threads finally, to clear them.

Make a hardwood adapter which screws nicely into the body and can be gripped into the three jaw for completing the turning of the base. Make an ivory stopper for the bottom hole with countersink to fit. Polish the inside surface of the stopper so that when screwed firmly home, it looks perfect inside. Screw

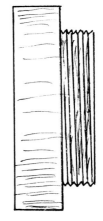

A hardwood adapter is used for chucking the bases, to complete turning

it in firmly and cut off carefully with the screever.

Finish the body on the hardwood adapter, skimming the stoppered base flush, and giving the whole a fine, lustrous finish with skilfully applied 'old fine' glasspaper and Brasso afterwards.

I now make 24 scallops with the vertical cutting frame, using the bead tool I mentioned, after sharpening. My vertical cutting frame can approach close to the chuck. With the wide pattern vertical cutting frame, you must chuck the body by the base.

This is the only ornamentally turned part of this project, except for a little at the top. Next you'll turn the matching body, following exactly the same process, but with much more care as it is so easy to turn a bit more than you intended and mar the similarity of the pair.

Of course, unless the curvilinear apparatus is used, they may vary, but exact replicas are normally either machine-made or moulded, and of course, it is the tiny variations that constitute the charm of hand work.

CENTRE SECTION

Chuck by the top, turn and face. I have a tubular coring saw and can take out a core ¾in (19mm) diameter, otherwise the piece must be bored and opened to 1in (25mm). Chuck by the bottom, turn, face and complete the hole. Chuck again by the top. You can tighten the chuck without fear of bruising, because it

Centre section shaped and opened

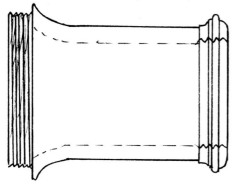

is at least ¹⁄₁₆in (2mm) oversize. Turn down the portion to cut the outside thread to fit the bottom section. I have the diameter at least ¹⁄₁₆in (2mm) oversize, and the tee about 1in (25mm) from the work.

I give the 20 chaser a rub on the stone, check that all is correct, and give the tee a rub with a candle. I drop the teeth right down to half past seven as I describe my little clockwise circles, and confidently, but so lightly, strike the thread as the chaser moves to the left. Keep it on the move for, if you allow it to pause, it will cut a series of rings, not a screw. It's a knack any persevering person can acquire. Set the lathe speed to suit yourself; 100–400rpm will be okay.

If your thread is faulty, turn down and try again. If true, do not chase it down to size, as too much chasing can lead to drunkenness. Turn it down with a flat tool, leaving enough thread to guide the chaser until you get a good fit with the body. I make a tiny clearance against the shoulder with a thin screever (parting tool) so that the body will screw right home. Then I open the inside like a bell, with an inside tool (Holtz right side tool), glasspaper and Brasso.

Make another hardwood adapter in the shape of an internally threaded ring, which is gripped in the three jaw to hold the centre section. The great advantage of these three jaw adapters of course, is that you can tap the work true in a trice, and it takes so very little time. So don't let a single day pass without a few minutes practice with the chaser: it's the 'open sesame' to real turning!

Screw the centre section on the adapter good and tight and do your turning lightly. Face it to the pre-determined length, and open the recess for the screw a bit less than the required diameter, and at least ¼in (6mm) deep. There is no need to leave a shoulder for your inside chaser to jar against. A small round tool removes that shoulder and tapers it into the main hole.

Cut a sound inside thread – 20 again. Clean up inside, and Brasso. Finish the outside turning to ornamental standards, and Brasso. Repeat the lot for the second centre section.

TOP

Turn cylindrical to the correct diameter and face the ends to the right length. Grip the top end in the three jaw – tight as you like as it has to be rounded later. Turn the end down for cutting the external screw to fit the top of the centre section, about ⁹⁄₃₂in (7mm) long, and cut another screw to fit perfectly – just like that!

Turn the guidelines for the holes, using the tiniest cutting frame bead tool – it's about ¹⁄₃₂in (1mm) – to give a bead at the top and bottom 1in (25mm) apart.

Hollowing out the top section

Home-made tool used with the armrest, for turning the inside of the top

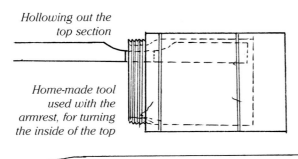

The interior is turned next, as shown in the illustration above, the hole ending about ⅛in (3mm) beyond the top bead. The wall is about ⅛in (3mm) thick. I made a tool to do this. If you make two marks on the tool to observe how far forward and back it must go, you'll find it quite accurate.

I made the final cuts with this tool after I'd drilled a couple of holes, as the wall must be thin enough to allow sugar through without clogging.

There are five panels of holes around the top, so I used the same bead tool to cut five upright lines between the boundary beads with the horizontal cutting frame, taking care not to allow them to cross. This, of course, is not limited to ornamental turners for, in the

absence of such shameless luxuries, I should simply pencil in five accurate lines, fix a vee tool in the three jaw, cut them by hand (with the tool going at top speed) and you'd hardly notice the difference! You haven't a vee tool? Tush! Knock one up out of a large nail (with a small three square file).

Now we come to the most delightful part of the whole piece – the drilling of the holes and the spiral incising. Firstly, while the top is revolving in the lathe, pencil seven equidistant lines between the boundaries, by eye. Mark the middle line first, then a middle line on each side: four more middle lines and you are there.

Take it out of the chuck, sit down and mark the 18 holes in each of the five panels. First, mark four holes plumb in the middle of lines 1, 3, 5 and 7. These four holes mark the corners of six squares, three left and three right, so, mark in the four outer holes on the left and four on the right so that, together, they make six squares.

You can now put a mark in the centre of each square, i.e., two holes on lines 2, 4 and 6. You will now have 18 symmetrical points and can easily pencil in the spiral lines for incising.

I know there are ornamental turners who might shudder at the idea of passing up an opportunity of doing all this with the slide rest, drill spindle and spiral apparatus: I applaud those with brains to accomplish it and congratulate those with time! I hope they'll forgive me if my method sounds appalling, but I am

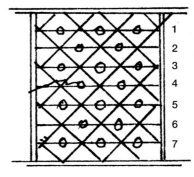

Marking out the pattern for the holes

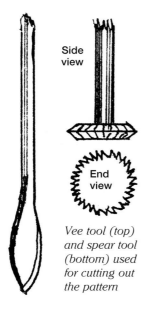

Side view

End view

Vee tool (top) and spear tool (bottom) used for cutting out the pattern

strictly limited in maths, time and patience and have always regarded the hand and eye as the finest and most adaptable tools in the world, making their use infinitely versatile. I find that hand work goes so well with ornamental turning, and I choose to work with unrestricted freedom rather than be hog-tied with rules. But please! If you have methods you prefer, do not let me lead you astray!

To continue, with a point tool, make a precise indentation at each marked spot – all 90 of 'em – and drill all the holes with a ⅛in (2mm) spear drill clamped in the three jaw, carefully pressing each indentation against the drill accurately, by hand.

You may be awe-stricken at the bare idea of incising the spiral lines freehand, but don't be fooled by that! It's easier than you'd imagine, using the vee cutter.

Grip a 3 or 4in (76 or 102mm) nail truly in the three jaw by about half its length, and shape the revolving head with a file. Then, with a small, three square file, cut the teeth. If carefully done, you'll have a nice little vee cutter: ⅜–½in (10–12mm) diameter will be fine.

Now for some practice. Mark similar lines on a cylinder of hardwood or plastic. Set the tool rest 4in (100mm) or so back to support the hands, and move the work against the cutter, making contact upon it where the arrow shows, with the speed of cutter at least 2,000rpm.

Hold the workpiece at the precise angle to allow the cutter to sail along the line. Relax! – you'll enjoy this. You should learn a lot in five minutes, but don't attempt to do the real piece

until you are confident. If you don't cross a boundary line or skid into a hole it will look fine! Mine does – even though I did skid into a hole! You know, an artist who uses a ruler every time he wants a straight line seldom improves his picture.

The holes should be very slightly countersunk from the inside. I used a tiny modelmaker's drill, like a dentist's, but it will be okay so long as they are cleaned up.

Make another adapter – they only take three minutes – to screw the top section into, so that the end can be turned to shape, and a hole bored and tapped for the finial. You can be as ingenious as you like in arriving at a design for the finial, as long as you're confident you can make another identical one.

NEVER be shy of taking what you want from every source of inspiration and adapting to your own fancy

In practice, I usually duplicate each process for the pair as I go along, and if the screws are not always interchangeable, they can be used on the same adapter. If not, I make another adapter, or alter the same one.

There were nine entries for the competition, with at least three other superb designs. Mine, being all ivory, had the edge I suppose, and the snag about winning is that the Worshipful Company retain the sifters that win for their dinners – ouch! I'd intended to give Dennis first refusal for a rare old remuneration! I shall keep the prototype though.

I should mention that for Worshipful Company of Turners' competitions today, ivory is barred and, incredibly, so are man-made materials such as the excellent alternative ivory/polyester resin. When the last tree has been consumed – give 'em time – I'm wondering exactly what . . . or shouldn't I ask?!

Chapter 12 ● *The* Question *of* TASTE

*I*sn't design a complex subject? I think if you have to explain it, or go into the intricacies of rules and mathematics, with thinly veiled insinuations that those who do not understand it must be ignorant, your case has already failed.

Any art must be articulate, someone wisely said. Another said, 'There is no such thing as significant art; there is art, and but little of that!'. Ah, but what does old Bill say? Art or design is related to taste, and of course each person is his or her own arbiter, which is why we can hardly criticize others.

> ## AS WE can't please all any more than we can offend all, why not please ourselves and make what we jolly well like?

We are not born with taste, but sort of grow into it, and either set like cement in whatever has become acceptable, or train our taste and try to keep it malleable and fair, refusing to condemn those who differ, because the world of creation caters for all tastes, austere, dignified, or quirkish and undignified – and all shapes in between.

I try never to condemn another turner's work, 'orrible though I may regard it, because I know the maker at least must have liked it, done his best and even put it on display to show he confidently supported it. It is not kind to condemn a well-meaning work, more especially because your own work will almost certainly be rated poor and tasteless by some others, and rightly so, because we all vary so much.

Of course, it may be thought there is a safe area of design which is incapable of displeasing anyone because it is lively without going over the top, and at the same time dignified without being boring. But in truth, there is no area so safe, but that some will hate it. Therefore, as we can't please all any more than we can offend all, why not please ourselves and make what we jolly well like?

INDIVIDUAL STYLE
The inexperienced, who may not have settled for any particular genre, may be well advised to take the safe course and follow whatever is successful – if anything ever is – but sooner or

Left *Two old ivory pieces from Bertram's piscatorial chess set* later he will, hopefully, steer his own path and seek individuality. Then he will find out whether or not to continue on that path, because the criterion is, of course, 'Can you earn your living at it?', and it's no good carrying on making 'masterpieces' which will only be recognized as such 100 years after your demise!

Of course, there must be countless turners working for pleasure, regardless of profit, and they really can please themselves. Their only limitation is the space they have to store their output. The answer here is – keep it small.

ORNAMENTATION

Ornamental turnery is a thorny subject where design is concerned. Many of the samples illustrated in books seem uncomfortable: I mean, they are often crude, shapeless pieces upon which embellishment has been wrought for no more reason than because the rare and complex instruments of torture exist!

One famous turner deliberately set out to use every possible piece of ornamental turning equipment on a chess set. Using the curvilinear apparatus with the spiral ditto, Atkinson's reciprocator, ellipse, rose engine etc., ad nauseam, he concocted a set I wouldn't dare to criticize. Why? Because he regarded it as one of his finest achievements – and beauty is in the eye of the beholder, especially when it's his baby!

Another equally famous turner declared – to me – it was the ugliest set he'd ever seen, but I'd say that was a sour grapes opinion. I must admit, I admired it, and so did many others,

The Antithesis of Homogeneity.

Success in art! What yardstick measures this?
The greatest triumphs of the turner's skill
May halt us, overawed with wonder & respect,
As though we stood within Jehovah's walls
Agazing at some high magnificence.

They stand with dignity, self-satisfied,
As if aware that those who gaze at them
Would surely never dare to pick them up!
But pass on chastened & a whit dismayed,
Perhaps a trifle humbled in their art.

Success it is – that noble monument
So faultless in its flowing lines – and yet
Success of different genre attracts me more,
A work that causes not the pensive look
Or brings the anxious frown of serious thought.

Upon the show stand rarely may be seen
Oft dwarfed by lordly works of which I spoke
A brief respite from sombre, showy things
A piece that brings a sparkle to the eye,
Perhaps an exultation of delight!

Some genius has 'wrested from the muse'
A strange new work that in its novelty
Arrests the glance – we want to take it up
And handle it, admiring its quaint charm,
Or damning its creator for a fool!

Small matter either way – as long as thought
And skill of high degree have fashioned it
The int'rest that it draws proclaims its worth,
Imparts encouragement to all who see
And have the wit to recognize a gem.

The charm of such delightful rarities
That stand amid the mighty & prevail
Like diamonds upon a shingle beach
Is oft the outcome of the merest chance
And gives the "Tally-ho!" to all who turn.

For who could value treasure by the ton?
It is the simpler charm of matchless things,
Which only the discerning comprehend,
That brings this life of ours rich piquancy
And sends us to our lathes with fresh resolve.

even if it did seem uncomfortable. And anyone could appreciate that it took far more skill, experience and time than most turners could ever contrive to muster on one piece of work.

Holtzapffel Volume 5 examples do not look uncomfortable – they look good and very self-satisfied; offend or please! All the superlative pieces were made by turning wizards to show the possible and the impossible (you better believe it!) capabilities of the machinery.

Undoubtedly they were well designed, far beyond the ability of an ignoramus like me to begin to produce. They were meant to show how far you could go, and if they went miles too far for some to appreciate, let them not complain that they were kept ignorant of the wonderful potential of all the many and various accoutrements.

If I didn't personally like the pieces, ignorance alone would render me dumb, but, dammit, I have to like them! The workmanship is so impeccable, and yet the crude type of ornamental turning can well put people off the art.

SUCCESSFUL DESIGN

I have expressed my feelings on success – or otherwise – in art with some verses I've just revised and rewritten after 20 years. As you can deduce, I had one or two pieces in mind representing the strange new works 'wrested from the muse'. Years ago in the Society of Ornamental Turners, we had a member named Jowett (yes – from the family of the famous car of that name) and he was one of the really imaginative ornamental turners whose brain was a natural for the subject. Not only did he produce works of taste and beauty, but on the odd occasion he'd turn out pieces

of whimsical delight that defied emulation. Orthodox he could never be!

COMPETITION

Mr Jowett put up a special medal to be competed for biennially. I had never hazarded an entry for this award up to now, but recently I had a small repair to do on, of all things, an ivory ear trumpet.

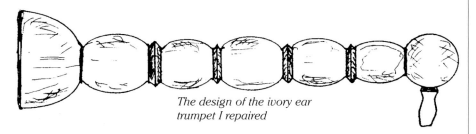

The design of the ivory ear trumpet I repaired

It was made in half a dozen joined pieces, one of which was missing and another to be replaced. When I'd done the job, I couldn't resist trying my hand at an ornate one, simply because it was such an unusual subject. I sorted out some ivory from my box of small points, donkey's years old, and just let nature take its course.

TURNING THE EAR TRUMPET

The trumpet end came first. I rough turned it and cut an internal thread at either end, and made adapter plugs for securing it in the three jaw. With an adapter in the large end, I turned the trumpet, then cut flutes with the horizontal cutter.

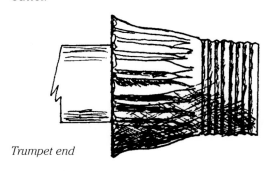

Trumpet end

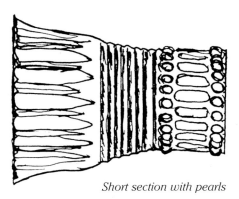

Short section with pearls

Next I turned a short section which screwed into the small end of the trumpet, and, with the drill spindle, I cut two rows of pearls, one each end, then made fine wide flutes between the pearls.

Section three was turned next, and screwed in with an outside thread cut on the other end, each section being bored with an accurate hole, commensurate with the outside diameter, but not less than ⁵⁄₁₆in (8mm).

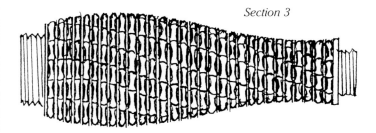

Section 3

Section 4

With the tailstock supporting the small end – the piece was now 5in (125mm) long – I cut a fine spiral of astragals along the whole shaped section. This is done by blacking over the piece with an ordinary lead pencil (black lead), and then cutting a series of 12 with the vertical cutter, using the 144 row on the division plate and just obliterating the black at the meeting points.

Start the next row of 12 immediately adjacent, beginning on hole number two, then continue along the shaped section, advancing a couple of holes for each row, 4, 6, 8, 10 etc., just taking out the black all the time, and being careful to keep the tool good and sharp.

Section four is turned with an inside thread at each end and is held for decoration with an adapter plug, and supported by the tailstock. Two rows of pearls (smaller than the first lot), separated by flutes midway between the pearls, are fashioned with the drill spindle. Black lead is used again while a similar spiral is made along the remainder of the section, using the same sequence of 12 segmental cuts per row on the 144, but this time using a narrow flat tool in the vertical cutting frame. Each row is adjusted to run immediately next to its neighbour, either by eye or by an automatic ratchet on the end of the main screw – if you happen to own one . . .

The final section is a short cylinder ending in a sphere. The male thread at the beginning is screwed into an adapter plug. I use whatever comes to hand for these adapters whether ivory, plastic or hardwood, and I keep a tinful of assorted ones.

Using the drill spindle, I begin with a third lot of pearls and flutes – the

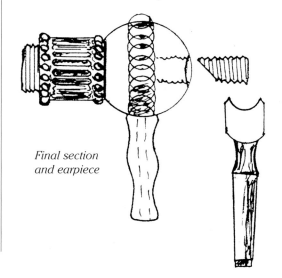

Final section and earpiece

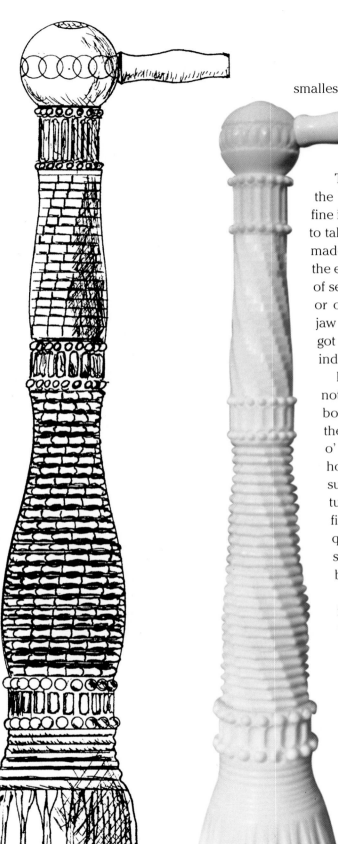

smallest set of the three – then, using a bead drill, cut a row of barley corns around the circumference of the ball.

The sketch, bottom left, will explain the boring. A hole right through, with a fine inside thread cut in the top of the ball to take a screwed plug. A screwed hole is made in the side of it to accommodate the earpiece. I am sure you will find a way of setting it up accurately in some chuck or other. I fooled around with the four jaw chuck and bits of old glasspaper till I got it right, but I must say, a four jaw independent would have been easier.

Fit the screwed plug in nicely, but do not cut it off until you've slanted the bottom end 45°, to move the sound in the right direction (if it makes a ha'p'th o' difference – which I doubt!) Screw it home with a dab of adhesive, making sure the slant faces the earpiece, then turn it flush. The buff makes a really fine job of the whole piece. It is a quirkish item and right up Mr Jowett's street to be sure. And I only wish he'd been there to see it.

It failed of course – perhaps because it was thought to be a flower holder, though who ever heard of anyone sticking a flower holder in their ear? It was past president George Corderoy (the famous George of the Bailey) who told me that the best hearing aid was an ear trumpet. Pardon . . . !

The finished ear trumpet

Chapter 13
Turning BONE

Bertram in action

Bertram's 5 x 5ft pantry workshop

T he bones mainly used in the turning trade were the buttock and shin bones of beef cattle, ox and calf. I can remember the old chipping block outside the shop – talking about the 1920s now mind – where bones were trimmed at the ends to fit the cup chuck.

The necessary boiling of the bones to extract the oil and marrow makes them ulitmately more brittle, but only by boiling and keeping them moist is it possible to turn them at all.

Bertram had a team of half a dozen turners making one-piece and two-piece screwed shaving brush handles. When turned, they

Left Zebrano powder bowl with polyester resin inlay

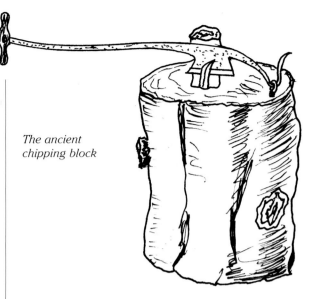

The ancient chipping block

were soaked for a day in turpentine, then boiled in water for an hour or so to make them white. They were polished with pumice powder and water, applied on a piece of felt. Polishing compos used for ivory and plastics were unsuitable for buffing bone which, being porous, would quickly fill up with unsightly spots all over.

In my teens, in the 1930s, I had the occasional job of hiring a coster's barrow (four old pence an hour – worth a couple of quid in today's apology for money!) and pushing it about 6m (10km) from Dalston to Clapton and back to collect a few sacks of bone strips from the toothbrush manufacturers. These strips would have been ideal for lace bobbins; I should think leg bones rather than round shanks would be best.

We cut the bone on a 6–7in (150–175mm), 22 gauge (1mm) circular saw, mounted on a hand-turned and screwed boxwood arbor. When I started my very own turning shop in the Lower Clapton Rd in 1947, Bertram bought me half a hundredweight of lignum logs, of 2–3in diameter (51–76mm) – mainly sapwood from Waterman & Ross in the Old Ford Rd.

I've heard it mentioned that wood chucks have to be regularly trued up due to warpage. Recently I unearthed an old saw that hadn't been used for at least five years. It ran as true as the last time I used it, if not truer. A good bit of timber that was.

The saw table was also fashioned by us out of a piece of mild steel about 3 x 7 x ½in (75 x 175 x 12mm), and set up in the pedestal of the tool rest. With this nice little saw you can cut bone and ivory in lengths and cut them roughly round.

Start the bones by sawing off the knuckles, which are too porous for use. The end section will

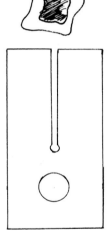

Cross section of beef leg bone

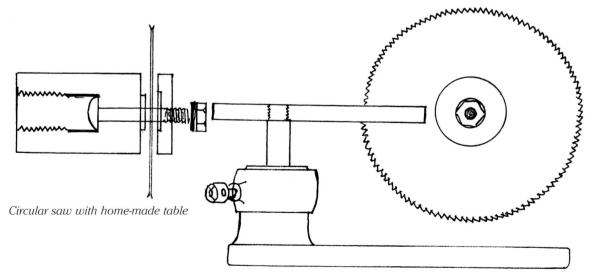

Circular saw with home-made table

reveal where the meat of the bone is and several pieces of rod may be cut from each one, care being necessary to cut them straight.

It is not too difficult to keep a saw in good condition if a few simple points are understood. You will need two or three 5in (125mm), single cut, three square saw files and a shaded table lamp. Normally I have six or seven handsaw teeth to the inch.

STRIKING

With the saw in motion, lay an old saw file on the saw table, then carefully and very slowly bring it up to the saw very lightly so that the teeth hiss on the flat of the file – not the corner – for a couple of seconds while the file is held perfectly still.

Stop the saw, and with the lamp shining from the left and yourself standing on the right, the points of the teeth that have been struck will appear as bright points of steel. Holding the saw firmly in the left hand, take a good file and, observing the bright points as they appear one by one, file the front and back of each struck tooth until the bright point just disappears. The file must be held horizontally and parallel with the mandrel.

Drop it lightly into the tooth so that it fits snugly without wobble, then lower the handle about 5°. This is the filing angle, which must be held consistently. Let the file cut without forcing, and remove it on the return stroke. If less than half of the teeth have been struck, give the saw another strike with the old file and file up the struck points again.

CROSS FILING

The next step is to give each tooth one stroke with a well worn file, in the opposite direction, i.e., from left to right with the left end of the file lowered slightly. This file is used quite lightly and without a handle. It is held by the point and pulled to the right, while watching to make sure the file maintains the correct angle consis-

tently – the tang always slopes downwards and fits well into each tooth. A bad filer can be clearly heard in a busy shop. A common fault is to use about 3in (76mm) on a 5in (127mm) file. Using only part of the file when rhythmically filing a saw is short-changing on the stroke, the same as not following through with the whole arm movement in swimming. The tooth is not properly filed and is likely to be uneven, and the file is worn unevenly. Saw doctoring is a skill that must be learnt and good filing is a great asset and shows in the result. I learnt it at St. Ives, Cornwall where I worked for a time in the ivory piano key trade.

> # IT IS not too difficult to keep a saw in good condition if a few simple points are understood

The saw should now be in good condition for cutting. There are more technical processes used, but for the occasional user it is better to strike lightly, file and cross file as described, whenever necessary. Inexperienced saw filing usually tends to produce some unevenness in the teeth, but unless very pronounced, this does not impair the saw's efficiency noticeably.

Unevenness can be avoided or corrected by observing the shape and size of each tooth as it comes, and by filing to correct the errors. An uneven saw is gradually corrected over a number of filings. Two essential requirements are care and common sense.

There is value in acquiring a rhythm when cross filing a saw, but do not sacrifice accuracy for speed. A speed of 180 strokes a minute is strictly for professionals. For the amateur, 100–120 strokes is a good rate. This, of course, doesn't apply to filing up the points after striking, which must be done with precision however long it takes.

SAWING

When sawing bone or ivory, oil is brushed little and often on each side of the teeth with the saw in motion, using the left hand for the left side and the right hand for the right side. Never cross over the saw with your hand. Steer the material carefully and without force, withdrawing it swiftly from the saw and advancing as carefully again to clear the kerf.

Burnt dust will adhere to the sides of the saw, especially if not enough oil has been used. This is best scraped off with a handy sliver. If burning and binding are excessive, slightly more set will be required, but don't overdo this, and always set your own saw for saw doctors don't usually understand our saws.

The ivory saw has no guard, but with my foot control the saw is in motion only when sawing is in progress, and this is a safety measure that promotes confidence. When I began sawing for the first time I was nervous, but I quickly gathered confidence sawing boxwood into thousands of catheter plug blanks. The only time I was in any danger was when I became over-confident, so I never fail to have the greatest respect for my sharp friend, the circular saw. Our sawn pieces are then hubbed to fit the chuck, whether round or square (for lace bobbins).

WORKING WITH BONE

The vital part comes next. The bones are boiled for an hour or so in water, then kept in water while you are using them. My way was to put a dozen or so on the bench and cover them with a damp cloth. Thus prepared, bone is very pleasurable to turn with gouge and square tool.

When making lace bobbins I used to turn them in a small, three jaw between centres, but a nicer way is in a square hole chuck. These can be bought – some turners are always buying things! – but a small cup chuck, plugged with boxwood, drilled the appropriate size and

filed into a slightly tapered square, will not only amply fill the bill, but also save you money for something useful!

When turning bone, I think anything between 1,800 and 2,800rpm quite suitable for lathe speed, and for bobbins as high a speed as possible, though I have never had the opportunity of trying at higher than 3,000rpm.

Fashion the bobbin in whatever pattern you choose to devise, but leave the slender part at the top to be turned separately in the three jaw. You may prefer to finish it in one, but I found this easier because there is firmer support, and you can finish the fiddly bit at the top delightfully, and then turn down the stem with a keen, small, flat tool, tilting it skilfully to get a nice, slender-waisted shape.

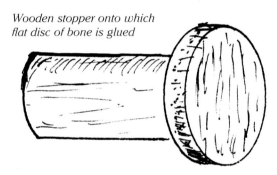

Wooden stopper onto which flat disc of bone is glued

Bone turning is all spindles and hollow ware – there is no solid stuff. Boxes and shaving brush handles were all stopped at the ends with flat discs cut from suitable bone, glued on wood stoppers and gripped in the three jaw – or tapped into a cup chuck.

Escritoires (delightful Lovejoyish word!), cabinets, chests, etc., in the days of fine furniture, before the turners had died out, simply bristled with cabinet knobs made of bone or, more often, ivory. Nearly always they

Two-piece cabinet knob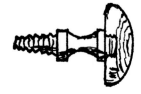

were made in two pieces, necessarily so in the case of bone, because solid bone over ½in (13mm) in diameter is not to be had. In the case of ivory, not only is it no saving of time for an ivory turner to make knobs out of the solid, but it is positively wasteful because small spindle ivory and flats came out of the waste, but solid stuff was expensive.

I had one question put to me; '. . . how were these knobs turned, in particular the internal screw threads, since there seems to be no room for a chaser?' A wry smile flickered over the ancient visage as I pictured someone grinding down a new and fiendishly expensive chaser until it was small enough to be used in such tiny holes!

Two-piece collar stud

In the trade, of course, old chasers gradually got ground away to almost nothing. Old chasers actually never die – they fade away and are still kept for the odd job or even used for turning tools, for old turners waste nothing. An ancient, tiny chaser is more valuable than a new one on some of my work. The acme of this tiny thread chasing used to be making two-piece bone collar studs on the treadle lathe. They got one and tuppence a gross a century ago, but that equates with at least 12 quid today. Don't ask me how they did it! If I were asked to make them, I'd quote a pound each. But before the days of plastics, when so much was made by hand, the ability and speed of these craftsmen was awe-inspiring, though not to be wondered at because the secret was 'quality first – speed will come later'. If it didn't, it could mean the loss of a job because fine craftsmen were not scarce in those days, and competition was fierce.

SCREW CUTTING

I do lots of turning and screw cutting close to the jaws of three and four jaw chucks. Two considerations make this quite safe:

1 I round off the sharp edges of the jaws on the grindstone and file the outer entrances of the slots through which they slide, so that danger and lacerations are minimized.
2 My left hand is never above the tool or in danger of being pushed into the jaws by the movement of the tool to the left.

The fingers of the left hand are below the tee – they can never be caught between the jaws and the tee rest, and if the jaws touch them at all, the rounded edges are harmless. Only the left thumb on top of, or at the left side of the tool, would seem to be vulnerable, but the thumb is in control and keeps clear of the jaws, you bet! Even when woodturning with jaw chucks you do not allow fingers above the tool rest when moving close to the jaws.

There is a third consideration in doing small work very close to the jaws and that is speed, which is usually quite slow. For tiny screws I often come down to below 100rpm. Of course, I do have foot-controlled variable speed which makes all things possible.

CABINET KNOBS

For cabinet knobs I start with the heads, cutting as many discs as I need from flats, barks, can-waste, etc., just as it will cut, and usually plank grain which is not the slightest disadvantage. Bone of course, if bone is used, has no grain at all.

Using the small circular saw, with its fine, thin teeth, I can cut round corners and trim these rounds quite easily. I also cut the stems from whatever I can find; usually cans, but these are all lengthways of the grain as most spindle turning must be.

Start turning by centring the disc in the three

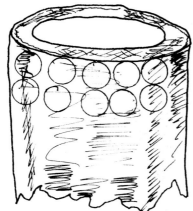

End of tusk, known as 'can-waste'

Flat, 'barky' ivory waste

jaw. I could cut an inside thread in a shallow, flat-bottomed hole – using the armrest of course – but I find it simpler to tap the thread with a sharp plug tap in a handle.

On my lathe I can run the belt backwards by hand. In fact, I can also run it forwards by hand, carefully, when tapping, because it is very easy to strip the thread in such a shallow hole. Should that happen, I cut another thread with an inside chaser, of necessarily larger diameter.

Plug tap, with handle

The next job is very pleasant, namely, to turn the heads to shape on an adapter plug gripped in the three jaw. Such a plug is simply made of brass, ivory or even casein plastic or similar. I cut the thread the same size as the tap of course. The turning is done with my long-handled ³⁄₃₂in (2.5mm) round nose tool, a square tool and a point tool.

Brass arbor

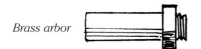

Turn it roughly to shape with the round tool on the armrest. With the square tool, turn down to the correct diameter plus ¹⁄₃₂in (0.5mm) to allow for rounding with point tool and papering. Get the thickness right and make a nice dome with the square tool.

There are unlimited varieties of shapes and decorations on cabinet knobs, but perhaps the most widely used are those done with an outside chaser, about 24 teeth per inch, making a series of rings.

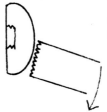

Head of knob

Side view   Plan view

The important detail in getting the knobs uniform is to have the centres right. That means the rings must begin at the same distance from the centre. Unless I am copying a pattern, my usual habit is to pencil a ring in the middle, about ⅛in (3mm) in diameter – by eye. Then, with the chaser flat on the armrest, I carefully place the extreme right hand tooth upon the near side of the pencilled ring.

Sloping the tool downwards, I press that first tooth into the pencil line, move the handle of the tool to the left, and watch the rings appear one by one as the teeth follow the curve of the dome, finishing wherever you wish.

Inscribing the pattern with a hand chaser

Now, although you know you are not cutting a screw thread, and you know jolly well that this is the simplest of jobs, yet, because the tool is a chaser, it may well try to jump out of its designated grooves: it does with me so it's bound to with you! The answer is to feed in very gently and stand no nonsense! You may prefer to make the grooves singly with a flat point tool, judging the sequence by eye.

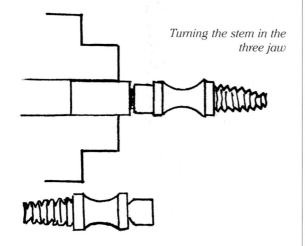

Turning the stem in the three jaw

The stems are done next, either with single pieces in the three jaw or using longer rods to make several, also in the three jaw. As the sketch above shows, the outside screw is turned first, unless you have decided to make it a plain dowel. In either case, make them all the same diameter, and parallel, close to the knob so that it can be gripped in the three jaw positively, for turning the fine screw that fits the head.

Now, you've got to cut this short thread up to a shoulder, so prepare it thus. As aforesaid, only the left thumb is above the tee – on top of the chaser. Your fingers are around the pedestal, the tee is no closer than 7⁄16in (12mm) from the work, and no higher than centre. The chaser comes up from below to cut, moving to the left with the lathe speed about 100rpm for these tiny screws. There's plenty of time to remove it before it jolts into the shoulder!

Two things – make the thread length twice as long as you need and trim the end when you've got a good thread that fits the head. And keep practising on any bits of hard material at odd moments. As old James Lukin wrote a century ago, ' . . . the skill will not long be wanting.' Further, don't forget to enjoy it. As Bertram always said, ' . . . some other fool's done it and so can I!'.

You may fix the head with a dab of adhesive, but I don't always. A strong finger and thumb around a piece of abrasive paper tightens them sufficiently. If you really need glue it's a sign of a duff thread and you don't want too many of those.

A good reason for making the dowel into a screw is that you can then screw each knob on a rod, with an internal thread to fit, so that you can polish them on the buff with less chance of them flying all over the shop. I like a good buff polish, but a finish in the lathe with Brasso on cotton wool is almost as good.

STAINING IVORY AND BONE

One reader wondered how to stain ivory or bone. After polishing, brush them in hot washing up liquid – detergent. Rinse in hot water and put them in hot water dye made from – what? That is the question. There are aniline water dyes made from chemicals if you can get them. Follow the instructions for mixing the amount you need in an old saucepan, add a few spoonfuls of acetic acid (which is referred to as vinegar in the fish shop) to act as a mordant.

Place your pieces in a chip frying sieve and move it about to obviate air bubbles, until the required colour is obtained. Take them out and rinse in hot, clean water, and leave to dry for a day. Polish with soft cloth or swansdown buff using fine white porthos compo.

There are natural dyes made from various plants and berries for those who may wish to pursue a more interesting and superior way of staining.

Chapter 14 ● *Chess Set:* ONIONS *and* BASES

Several years ago I made three sets of Indian-style chessmen, 7in (180mm), the step-by-step details of which I will cover here. As there cannot be many doing that sort of thing in today's world, I regard it as almost obligatory to set it down in chronological order, as I progress with a project that is undeniably the apogee of the turner's art.

As usual, I study examples of original sets and then adapt and modify in order to make them undoubtedly my own. This unashamedly avoids complicated and fiddly carvery that is outside my limitations because of being so time-consuming. The only people who could ever have lived on such work are the 'handful of rice a day' workers, and I somehow think today they are rather thin on the ground!

IVORY

Over the years I have accumulated a store of old ivory which usually covers my modest needs. It may be said that since ivory is a *verboten* substance we should forget it, but, as a material, ivory is like the great forests that are now on the way out if senseless mankind achieves his self-destructive purpose.

Finished pieces from the chess set

Left Parting off a king with the Holtzapffel parting tool

Properly conserved, both ivory and timber would forever yield more than man's needs, but greed, selfishness and the headlong rush to destruction threaten ruination of the earth, although 'tis but a temporary setback from which the earth will recover. The would-be destroyers will not!

The ivory that remains is still with us and is the most beautiful material for the craftsman. Even though we may never get any, there may yet drop into the lap of any one of us a chunk or two that someone has stored away. Ivory also holds sufficient interest to warrant writing about, so I make no apology.

Further, the notes are perfectly valid for wood and other materials. In fact, after I'd described these chess sets in the bulletin of the Society of Ornamental Turners, a member made a very good set in wood – an Everest achievement! And as a spur to those who do not, as yet (let the reader use discernment!), count screw cutting among their skills, this chap had joined all pieces without screws.

DESIGN AND ART

There is unlimited potential in chesspieces for design, beauty, ingenuity and the whole gamut of the turner's and carver's art: the best of it is you don't have to actually play the game! And suddenly, just when life is becoming humdrum and in need of enlivening, along comes a chess design you can enthuse over, and you are oblivious to the whole world as you embark on the engrossing creation of yet another masterpiece.

If it's good enough to make three sets, I know there won't be a single boring moment as I watch the work grow, and if I wasn't so – I very nearly said old, but belay that rubbish! – I'd actually resent any and every intrusion.

CUTTING LIST

Before sawing, it is essential to make a cutting list, but you can hardly begin until you've

made drawings of each of the pieces, viz, king, queen, bishop, knight, rook and pawn, on squared paper. Of course, you don't have to fool about making meticulous line drawings, but on squared paper – easily obtainable in cheap exercise books – you do get them symmetrical and to working dimensions. The

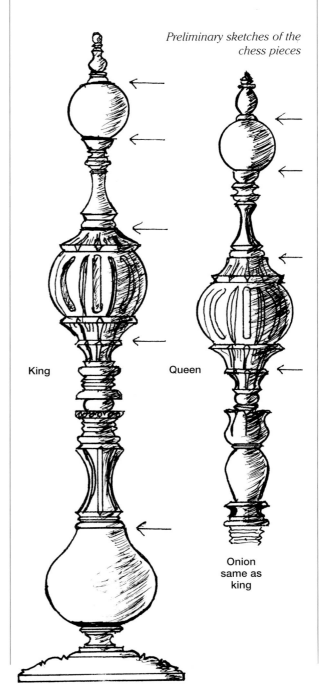

Preliminary sketches of the chess pieces

King

Queen

Onion
same as
king

shapes, also, are an approximation which only materialize when you turn them, for, to the turner, turning is easier than drawing!

In ivory, the set comprises 172 separate screwed parts. Three sets, plus six pieces extra as permanent patterns and show pieces, total 547 pieces, but for cutting there are fewer because you cut in lengths, taking the largest diameters first, working down to the smallest.

Obviously, you avoid cutting big stuff into small as far as possible. It is only by drawing each chessman and deciding exactly where the joins will be that you can plan your cutting list, which you alone will understand.

Although I'm making the king 7in (180mm), others may choose a different size. Ivory and bone may be sawn conveniently on a 6–7in (150–180mm), 22 gauge (1mm) circular saw. Nothing usable is ever wasted. Obviously, the wider the range of ivory stock, the more economical it is to cut chesspieces or anything else. In times past, when things were sensibly conserved and there was plenty of cheap ivory, it was never necessary to cut wastefully; you retained stocks and bought as required (and no order was too small!) from all types of cut sections. Now, we have to do the best we can from whatever we can scrounge.

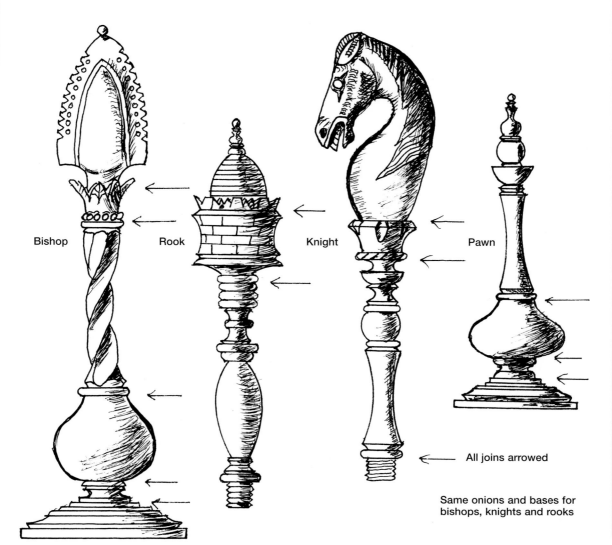

Bishop   Rook   Knight   Pawn

All joins arrowed

Same onions and bases for bishops, knights and rooks

TURNING THE ONIONS

The rough sawn cylinders are prepared for the chuck by hubbing the ends round on the big cutter or hub. As I do most of my turning in either a three or four jaw, self-centring, geared scroll chuck, I go through the whole of my ivory rods and prepare them on the hub.

I begin the actual turning with all the onions. Each one is fixed in the three jaw and turned smooth with a ⅜in (10mm) gouge, then faced and drilled – accurately, with the aid of the armrest. The hole is then tapped to ⁵⁄₁₆in (8mm) diameter with a 26 teeth per inch thread, about ⅜in (9mm) deep. As taps cannot be fully relied on to produce a uniform result, I always finish the thread to my requirements with an inside thread chaser.

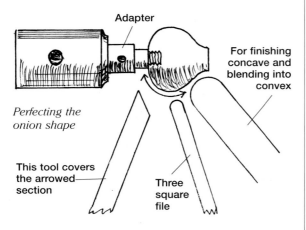

Perfecting the onion shape

I'm going to turn the onions on a brass adapter chuck in my Holtzapffel & Deyerlein Vampire lathe, dated 1813. (I always give the Vampire a plug as I'm immensely proud of that little 5in (127mm) screw mandrel headstock, which cost me £9.)

I make the adapter screw (with hand chaser) slightly larger than the ⁵⁄₁₆in (8mm) tap, because when I clean up the threaded holes with the chaser, it will enlarge the diameter slightly. I make each onion to fit that adapter. This includes the pawns. In the absence of brass for adapters I would use ivory, lignum or blackwood gripped in the three jaw.

I first turn it to the exact length, but a slightly larger diameter than the finished size, then drill and tap. For the royals (kings and queens) I use the same ⁵⁄₁₆in (8mm) tap, clearing with an inside 26 chaser and ensuring that the narrow face against which the stem will butt is faced to perfection.

I rough the onion to shape with a narrow round nose tool, then perfect the shape with an oblique tool and a round nose. Of course, without the use of the armrest, which comes into play throughout almost the whole of the finishing, I couldn't obtain the perfection upon which I insist – not that I am all that pernickety, but I have at least two hypercritical critics who will tell me! The only portion where the armrest is not used is that nearest the brass, where the oblique tool ensures that the bottom face of the onion is the same diameter as the brass to which it is screwed.

Where the front hollow blends into the convex part of the onion, I achieve an unbroken curve with a feather light touch of the larger round tool which needs to be ever sharp and well stoned – and all assisted by the armrest which obviates any tendency to jerkiness.

I don't mind what others say or do, there is no finer road to finished perfection in ivory on this sort of work than the aid of the 'the best turner in the trade', John Oakey, the glasspaper merchant; No. 1 grade, new and old. You might get it pretty good, but these curves will reveal tooling later if you don't watch it.

For the bishop, knight and rook onions I use a ⁹⁄₃₂in (7mm) x 26 tap for the front stem, and for the pawn onions I use a ¼in (6mm) x 26. I always keep my work in a covered box until I'm ready to polish it as unpolished ivory may crack, especially if there's a draught or it is in sunlight.

TURNING THE BASES

Next I turn the bases, starting with the royals. I do mine in a three jaw, but a cup chuck may be preferred. If you want to tap it in a cup chuck, prepare the piece in a three jaw, turning the end to a very slight taper which enters the cup chuck by about ⅟₁₆in (2mm) only. Several short, gentle, driving blows with a 1½lb (680g) ball pein hammer will fix it firmly and truly in the chuck, and it won't come out unless you are determined! Lack of confidence causes some to resort to glues or screws in cup chucks, but the only necessity is a rub of chalk.

I turn it to the right diameter and face, measure and mark the required thickness with dividers, then make a flat-bottomed hole, ³⁄₁₆in (5mm) deep, and tap with a ⁵⁄₁₆in (8mm) x 26 plug tap. Now, it's dead easy to bodge a job like this, so I'll show you how to succeed. Armrest, of course, then countersink with square tool. I imagine most turners use other methods when countersinking, but for accuracy there can be nowt better than the square tool on the armrest, which steadies and adjusts the tool exactly where you want it. You follow with a spear drill ³⁄₁₆in (5mm) deep, and open to a hole the right size for the tap, with a small inside tool. A D-bit, as illustrated below, opens already drilled holes to accurate diameters, with flat bottoms – most important for chess bases. D-bits also serve as reamers, but today they aren't easy to find: mine are all Holtzapffel ones.

Square tool from flat file

Narrow inside tool from three square file

D-bit (if you have one)

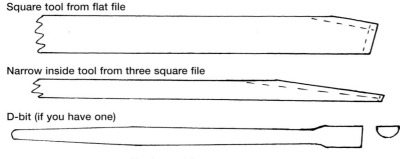

Tools used for counter-sinking

In a shallow hole it is easy to strip the thread and, in order to avoid this, I start a thread first with an inside chaser. This needs practice and a feather touch – don't force it – but even if you only partially succeed you'll find the tap,

having the ghost of a start, will advance without stripping. Clean the thread to the bottom by following with the chaser.

Incidentally, when taps get blunt, I sharpen the business side of each flute carefully on the corner of a fine grinding wheel, holding the tap perpendicular. The difference is gratifying.

TOOLS must be keen and applied lightly so as not to pick up the grain

The pattern on the surface is delightfully turned using the armrest (you can readily see why mine hangs under my arm permanently on a cord) with a round nose, a flat point tool and a thin flat tool. I use dividers on the armrest to mark off two appropriate places, but after the first couple only one mark is necessary because the eye is sufficient. You'll find they'll come out admirably if you give the tools plenty of drag – i.e., slope them down below centre – and a slow speed. Blunt tools are unacceptable and great care is needed in moving and placing them precisely. And don't forget to enjoy every minute – it's that good!

The best finish is obtained with Brasso on cotton wool, after judicious papering. After the first two or three, the rest will be no trouble at all. Part off with a screever, overall length about a foot, and use your solar plexus to advance the tool, as previously described.

You can't always find material of large enough diameter to furnish all the bases, so often they are cut from hollow sections which means plank grained ivory, but truly, they turn extremely well this way and have a better colour and lustre.

Tools must be keen and applied lightly so as not to pick up the grain. Each one has to be

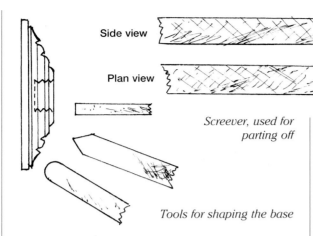

Side view

Plan view

Screever, used for parting off

Tools for shaping the base

chucked individually in the three jaw, base side out. Surface to finished perfection and turn as far as you can to finished diameter (or perhaps a little more). Reverse and fix carefully in the three jaw by just 1/16in (1.5mm) and complete. You may prefer the more comfortable spring chuck that has no jaws, but I'm so used to the three jaw with foot-controlled variable speed that I get little trouble.

CUTTING THE SCREW THREADS

The thread at least cuts better in plank grain. The tiny vee close to the jaws cannot be managed with the point or small flat tools so I contrive it using the screever, but for this I oilstone it first. I'll repeat that tools must be sharp, given bags of drag and placed precisely at properly controlled speed because, if you pick up the grain it shows.

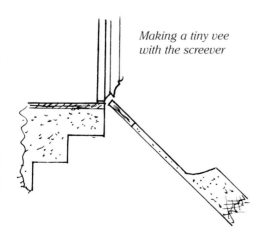

Making a tiny vee with the screever

The joining pieces come next. I turn all the studding to the correct diameter, then begin the first of the royals in the three jaw. Cut the thread to fit the base with no wobble. Turn a spigot for the onion thread and cut off. When all the bases have their joining screws, prepare an ivory adapter plug with an inside thread to fit the base screws. This adapter is held in the three jaw and tapped true as required for each joining screw, which is tightened and loosened with pliers (using glasspaper to protect the ivory). Turn a thread to fit the onion. If you make a small vee against the mating face with a point tool, quite carefully, the onion will screw on true.

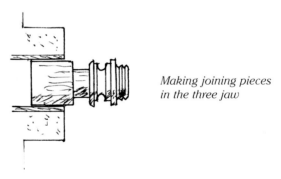

Making joining pieces in the three jaw

When all are done I finish the bottoms of the bases that need it by gripping the joining screws (in glasspaper) in the three jaw. I next polish each one on the calico mop, 8 x 1¼in (200 x 30mm) using Cannings Crown or Lustre compo. I normally polish as I go along. Buffs, of course, need to be worn in by use and a new one can be turned with an old scraper to make it nice and even, burning off the tags that appear with a lighted candle. Proper polishing has to be learned by practice; if you spoil the edges of the work, or get burn marks, don't blame the buff! Practise on something cheap –

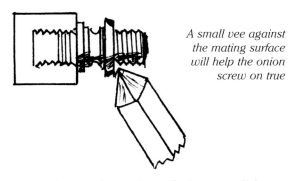

A small vee against the mating surface will help the onion screw on true

spare pieces of wood etc. I always polish my wood on the buff anyway.

TURNING THE PAWN STEMS

Now to make the charming pawn stems which, being long and slender, can be turned 'tween centres. But, my own way is to first turn them between centres merely to get them cylindrical, then turn them to shape in the three jaw, gripping each one half way to turn the delicate upper half, then gripping the screw end only to complete.

Why do it this way? Because, with the tailstock out of the way, I have more freedom and can achieve better results more easily. If there's more than one way of doing something I usually choose the easiest – which isn't always the quickest, especially in the preparation. The most striking example of this is my home-made variable speed device which takes a couple of days to make, but without which I'd be only half the turner.

I looked at the somewhat crude, home-made workings of the machinery in an old windmill recently. They reminded me of my back carriage and slipping belt, foot-controlled arrangement. I'm sure it's the homely efficacy and sheer friendliness of a craftsman's workshop that draws people like me to it on a Monday morning when ordinary folk would think of it as a disgusting bore!

The pawn stems, after the first two or three, take about 10 minutes each to turn beautifully. When a number have to be turned, like pawns, the work improves and the time is cut dramatically. The tooling becomes easier and is attended with more satisfaction. So – always welcome repetition work: it makes skillful turners.

To cut the thread to fit the pawn onion we need to make a split boxwood collet, bored so that the narrow stem can be secured and gently tapped true in the three jaw – or better still the four jaw if you have one. You'll soon get the hang of these collets and accumulate a tinful. If it doesn't go true first time try again, and always tap the collet, not the work. Polish the pawns, and that is the easy half of the set completed.

Split boxwood collet to hold the pawn in the three jaw

Chapter 15 ● *Chess Set:* Royal DECORATION

I intend to tackle the slotted balls for the royals in this chapter. The ivory is already prepared, but first I'd like a dummy run on something cheap as, with this, I'm going into the realms of the unfamiliar. Because of my experiments with old casein rod I can now set down the best method for success.

TURNING THE SLOTTED BALLS

Chuck by one end in the three or four jaw, turn it roughly cylindrical and drill half way, slightly below tapping size. Reverse in the chuck, meet the hole and, before you tap the thread (I'm using ⁹⁄₃₂in (7mm) x 26), hollow it out with a home-made tool as in the drawing, above

Above Ivory patterns for the Copenhagen/Tulip chess set, 6in (150mm)

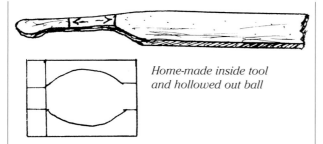

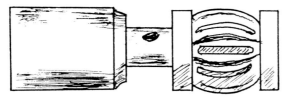

Home-made inside tool and hollowed out ball

right, using an armrest. Make sure you don't take out more material than is prudent.

If you make a couple of boundary marks as shown, you'll be sure to turn only between the arrows and get the inside barrel shape by feel. This makes less work for the slotting cutter and also avoids mutilating the thread, which I tap next and then chase a little with a 26 inside thread chaser, until it fits the brass adapter I have made, slightly bigger than the tap.

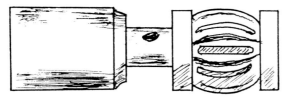

Slotted ball on adapter chuck

The two kings are a shade bigger than the queens and each process is repeated on all four as we progress. Screw the first onto the adapter and turn the ball as illustrated, without finishing the ends, but making them the correct diameters. Now I cut my slots on the ornamental lathe using the division plate and drill spindle. It's rather a strain on the slender drills which break when you least expect it, so we're going to do it the Compleat Turner's way, by pencilling the nine slots by eye and using a home-made slotting cutter like old Bertram. To obtain nine divisions by the way, put the ball in the three jaw, pencil a mark where the middle of each jaw touches, then simply mark two equidistant lines between each. QED (quite easily done).

The cutter is about $^{21}/_{32}$–$^{23}/_{32}$in (16–18mm)

diameter and $^{3}/_{32}$in (2mm) thick, with fine sawteeth; it was cut with care, but no special skill with a fine, three square file. If you make a hole in it, the arbor is easily contrived out of the hoard of bits and pieces, odds and coconuts of all materials every turner has. After many years the trick is to find the bit you know you have – somewhere!

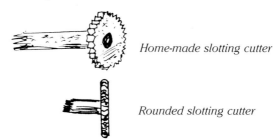

Home-made slotting cutter

Rounded slotting cutter

Nicer ends to the slots are obtained when the cutter is rounded instead of square, as shown above. Never begrudge the time spent making such cutters – they all have their uses to the turner/carver that every chess maker has to be. Before turning the ends, a little more hollowing may be done and this can be observed through the slots. I start by marking the slots in pencil carefully, and straight. Here we go now! The slotting cutter is clamped in the chuck, and running 2,000–3,000rpm, whatever you can muster.

The tee rest is 3 or 4in (76 or 102mm) back to support and steady your hands. The ball has a length of rod screwed into one end to hold it by, in the perpendicular position, but leave that there ball for the nonce! Instead, take an ordinary piece of wood and try cutting slots in it. You will quickly discover the special idiosyncrasies of the cutter – and yourself in relation to it!

Start on the ball only when you feel confident, then cut only one slot in each side; it is easier hollowing out the ball to the finish when there are only two slots. Stop the lathe frequently to observe the progress, and when the hollowing is complete (don't make it wafer thin – please!), you can cut the other seven slots.

It's time to make the thread in the other end of the ball, to fit the same adapter. The ends are turned to a concave, the top end a bit smaller in diameter than the bottom. I found when I'd turned the first end, that when reversed it was true enough to do the other, but, should it be untrue, screw it on an adapter plug in the three jaw, and tap it true with your trusty boxwood mallet. I regard the slotted ball as a 'nice' piece of turnery in the meaning of the word given in my old Chambers 'dic' – 'done with great care and exactness, accurate, dainty, agreeable, delightful.'

You will need two vee cutters to decorate – clamped in the three jaw. The first measures $^{21}\!/_{32}$in (16mm) in diameter and is $^3\!/_{16}$in (4.5mm) thick. I run the cutter at top speed, and with the ball screwed onto a rod to provide good hand control, make a deep vee midway between the slots, from north to south and into the ends.

Vee cutter

In a separate operation, put the same vee on the concave ends, but only two-thirds of the way up. To complete the decoration on the ends, use a fine nail vee cutter and make three fine lines between each pair of big vees. My sketches, below, should explain all. Notice the top has a slightly smaller diameter.

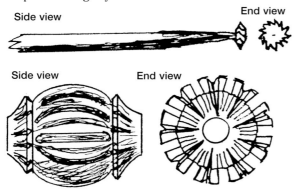

Vee cutter and slotted balls

TURNING THE STEMS

Next, the king stems, joining the onion to the slotted ball: all plain sailing. Grip about 1in (25mm) in the three jaw, cut a thread to fit the ball and turn the top part, then reverse, protecting the work from bruising by lapping glasspaper round it, and complete, turning the bottom thread to fit the onion.

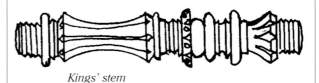

Kings' stem

You can do as you please with the shape of the first one – you are the designer – but the other king will have to match. On the shallow hollow I make six flutes with a small, rounded cutter made from a 3in (75mm) nail. You may pencil the lines precisely on the hollow, taking the positions from the three chuck jaws. The middle decoration has eight vees around the top, with eight drilled indents between them. The top decoration consists of 10 small vees coming two-thirds down from the top.

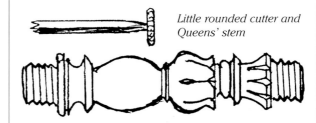

Little rounded cutter and Queens' stem

The queen stems differ from the kings as shown above, but are turned in the same manner and decorated with vee cutters. These vees are dead easy to make and you are bound to end up with lots of all sizes if you do much of this work.

THE TOP BALLS

My next job is the top balls – $^5\!/_8$in (15mm) diameter for kings and $^9\!/_{16}$in (14mm) for queens. From a short rod in the three jaw, turn it to an approximate sphere, but slightly oversize. You can get it quite accurate by applying a steel tube, oscillating it lightly from side to side over the pencilled ball until the black is removed. My tube (I have a few more of course!) was made from a short length of gas pipe, 21⁄32in (16mm), carefully turned inside to 17⁄32in (13mm) diameter, and angled down with a graver to almost meet the inside.

To get it sharp I move an oilstone across the front – slightly angled to touch the rear part only – when it is revolving slowly, then lightly remove the burr with the inside tool. It's only mild steel and you must keep it sharpened rather than try to force it and burn the material. Bore the ball about half way, and cut an inside thread about 3⁄16in (5mm) x 32 – or use a small tap.

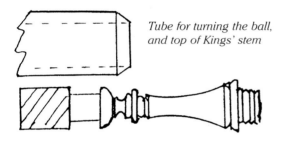

Tube for turning the ball, and top of Kings' stem

This is the top stem that screws into the top of the slotted ball. Having turned thus far in the three jaw to fit the ball, it is screwed into a female adapter plug, clamped in the three jaw, tapped true and tightened.

The other end is then threaded to fit the ball. This is tiny work for some, and you do need a lathe well under control, preferably by foot, but I am at my best at such work and get the utmost pleasure from it.

The 32 chaser is an easy one to use, but, sadly, it is only when they've been ground down over many years of work that the inside chasers are small enough to be used in tiny holes, so taps may be used in lieu of the inside chaser, and you will then need an outside chaser of the same thread, or you may try a die.

Often, I have considered the high cost of a pair of chasers and recommended several turners buy a pair between them and take turns practising. As soon as one becomes adept in their use he won't begrudge the cost of his own tools. But I can well understand that you need confidence first!

A spot of soap on the screw eases the ball on beautifully. All mine fitted truly – I was most surprised! While *in situ* I completed the top of the ball, drilled a 3⁄32in (2mm) hole and cut a 32 thread.

TURNING THE FINIALS

The best bit comes now. The finial on top of the ball is turned from any spare rods of ivory that will yield 1⁄4in (6mm) diameter. Turn the screw to fit the ball and cut it off the right length. You never know – it might go true, but not all mine do, quite.

Here's how to get the finial true. The prepared piece is screwed firmly into its ball. The stem, complete with ball and finial, is put in the three jaw, holding by the bottom screw of the stem – but very lightly. Get it running so that ball and stem are dead true, then pencil a spot exactly at the centre of the finial.

Remove, lap the ball with a trebled, narrow strip of old glasspaper to prevent bruising, but do not tighten the three jaw until the spot on the finial is made to run true. In carefully turning this tiny finial, a light touch is essential.

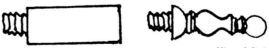

Kings' finial

For the queen stem and finial I wanted something different. I consulted the huge *Book of Ornament* (Franz S. Meyer), but to no

Queens' top stem and finial

avail, being overwhelmed by such a staggering array of excessive decoration. It's back to the pencil and envelope back. I came up with these, but whatever you draw, it always gets modified and improved in the lathe.

When working on tiny things, the eye is capable of reading to great accuracy. The only reason many of the antique sets varied so much in the facsimile turning, was not due to poor craftsmanship, but time and material. Bertram wrote to me on 3 April 1961, '... these old sets are looked on as "the work of the old masters which cannot be reproduced" – little do they know that the poor buggers got about sixpence an hour and worked about 10 hours a day and liked it ... it was good fun treading a lathe under a corrugated iron roof in temperatures up to 90°F (32°C), with the guvnor telling you what a B. fool you are, but you can learn a lot from these repairs. They are not beyond the capacity of chaps like you to reproduce. What they could do we can better, it's just a matter of price, and what was once a trade is now an art'.

The royals are complete and look magnificent now I've polished them.

THE BISHOPS' MITRES

The bishops' mitres I look forward to as a challenge because it's no job for a pessimist! As old Bertram said, 'If a man thinks he can't

do a thing, he'll be right!'. Quite a bit of 'hackery' is involved. Cutting the ivory in the rough shape and preparing it on the hub, or large cutter, it looks something like the sketches below.

The second two are what we're aiming at. The top part, which is hatched in the first sketch, is flattened with the cutter so that it can be gripped in the two or four jaw chuck. In the absence of such opulent luxuries, I'd bang a piece of boxwood into a suitable cup chuck, (NOT luxuries – necessities!), open it out to an appropriate taper, and tap the pieces into it, well chalked, with a 1½lb (680g), short-handled hammer, without the slightest bother!

Shape at bottom of bishops' mitre

If you pencil a line down the middle, and a dot in the centre of the base, you will ensure it's aligned correctly in the chuck. Face and drill not more than ½in (12mm) deep, and tap ⁷⁄₃₂in (5.5mm) x 24 – or what you will. Then, using an armrest and round tool, shape the bottom part of the mitre as shown above. Make them all the same curvature and diameter.

Use the long-handled, small, round nose tool very gingerly, or you'll jerk it out of the chuck – which is irksome after you've tapped the thread

Views of bishops' top

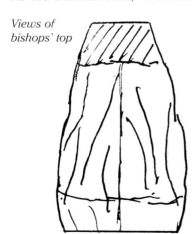

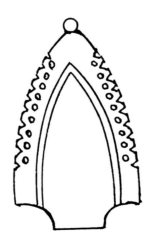

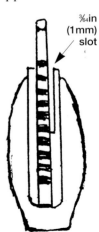

³⁄₆₄in (1mm) slot

because of the difficulty of replacing it precisely. My first one jerked out, of course, just to show me how to show you! The subsequent ones were drilled and tapped after shaping, to be on the safe side. Oops! There goes another!

I'll sharpen this round tool and apply it even more lightly. Of course, none will fly out if you spend enough time perfecting the flats where the chuck grips – but time is too valuable to squander on pernickety frivolities, and a turner needs some excitement in life!

The shape of the mitre is next turned, by screwing each one on a brass screw – either an adapter chuck or plug clamped in the three jaw. Turn it to the right length first and then use a stout round nose tool and square tool.

Coming to the tiny ball at the top, I use finer tools under the control of the essential armrest. As the tools are only contacting two edges, give them plenty of drag, i.e., way below centre height.

With a No. 10 outside chaser, make 10 vees on each side as shown in the sketch, bottom left, not sharp, and handle the chaser very carefully. If no chaser is handy, use a point tool, marking each vee carefully in advance.

Now comes the slotting. I use my 6¼in (6mm), 22 gauge circular saw and cut as shown in the illustration, right. Although I began nervously, I found it plain sailing, but handwork like this is attended with risk. Indeed, without risk little fine work can be done. I don't mean risk of injury to yourself, but to the work. You

Mitre slot

have to sail close to the wind sometimes, but the closer you risk failure the more satisfaction there is in winning through.

With the circular saw – or slotting cutter if you have one – you'll need to set the table quite low to get a straight cut. I don't know

how to tell you this, but it's best to be honest: now we come to the difficult bit! And those who haven't yet bought, begged, borrowed or pinched a hub will have to jolly well make one: about ½in (12mm) x 2in (50mm) diameter, with about 14 teeth per inch.

If you take so much trouble you will use it, and become more proficient with every practice session. You'll need to practise on something cheap. If you get a chance to watch a good spindle carver you will be impressed, but however good, hand cut work is crude, and it's the finishing of such work that rescues it.

When you have come half way near the result you visualized, then filed, scraped, papered and polished, you'll be so delighted you did it at all that your conceit will know no bounds! Success is commensurate with the time spent working at it. It's not a gift, it's all down to perseverance, but joyful perseverance I hope.

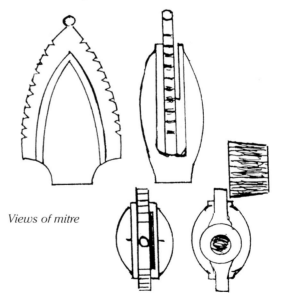

Views of mitre

The sketches above will give you an idea of the shape required. With the support of a rod which screws into the mitre, the piece is run down the small cutter lengthways, as shown. You must keep your eye on the cutter's edge to ensure you don't allow it to veer off in all directions.

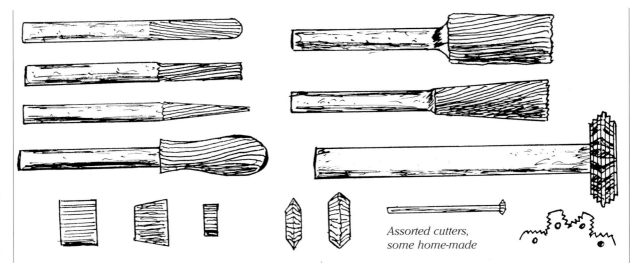

Assorted cutters,
some home-made

The round bottom section into which the support rod screws is blended and rounded into the shape of the mitre with the aid of a narrow, long cutter. The narrow mouldings are done with various fine cutters that can be unearthed, spotted and bought in the odd tool emporium and some catalogues. There's always room for one more! And where the cutters finish, the scrapers start, but they're no problem.

While all this is going on, do not think you are the only one who ever said, 'Oh dear! This is crude!', and can't see how it can turn out well. I've watched Bertram carving and coming to a bit that looks doubtful: 'Don't worry', he's said cheerfully, 'someone will like it!', and I seldom knew him get any work returned.

But work should never be judged at the half way stage. Time enough when it's done, and then you'll find, like me (hopefully), that your dismal forebodings were not realized and, if the work could have been better, it was still pretty good.

FINISHING TOUCHES

We're due for a fillip now because it's time for the vice work, when the rounded parts are perfected with the strips of glasscloth, and finishing touches can be done with scrapers. They look miles better already, but wait . . . the buff comes next. I use the edges of the buff for running down the mouldings, and the middle for the wide, rounded sides, running it downwards with the grain – but not fiercely so as to burn. Use polishing compo (Cannings Crown or the like) little and often.

After going over the whole, the rough places will be revealed. When all are done – not heavily – it's back to the vice with the scrapers. Usually I pencil the rough parts and then scrape out. The second buffing should make them perfect.

DRILLING

Risk is also involved in the last job of drilling. There are 10 vees on each side, so nine holes are required in each, between the vees – $\frac{1}{32}$in (1mm) diameter. Pencil a line close to the moulding on the outside borders, and make nine indents on each side, between the vees. Should you find the borders a whit too narrow to accommodate the holes without risk of breaking through the outside, you must take the mouldings back a little, by running down

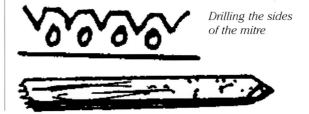

Drilling the sides of the mitre

the edge with a small cutter and scraping afterwards. You need a spear drill – not twist – but they're easily made with a small gas blowlamp, or without for such a simple job.

You need a fine drill that cuts without force, is not too delicate, yet makes holes no larger than ¹⁄₃₂in (1mm). Clamp the drill in the three jaw and feed the work to the drill, taking care not to go too near the outside edge or it could break through. Countersink both sides of each hole slightly, with a triangular point tool. Give a final polish, and then clean by immersing in hot water and brushing with an old toothbrush. I am highly delighted with mine and only a born critic will pick holes!

BISHOPS' STEMS AND NECKS

The sketches below illustrate the bishops' stems and necks. Turn the stem between centres, making a bead near each end – leaving room for the screws – and turning it slightly waisted in the middle. Turn each screw in the three jaw. It is ⁹⁄₃₂in (7mm) x 26 at the bottom, and ⁷⁄₃₂in (5.5mm) x 24 at the top. It is a four-fluted spiral and I mark it free-hand with an ordinary lead pencil (as the Weston brothers used to say).

No need to get technical in the marking: simply take the stem in your left hand – or right if you happen to be a port fin merchant – tilt it to about 70°,

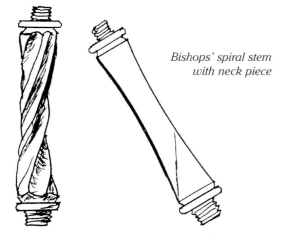

Bishops' spiral stem with neck piece

and pencil in the four spirals by keeping each line upright as you twist the piece evenly anti-clockwise, preserving the angle carefully. If you start them 90° apart, you must ensure they finish the same – the eye detects errors.

Cutting spirals calls for a cutter like the one shown right. Mine is 1⁵⁄₈in (40mm) in diameter, but it doesn't have to be as big. Run the cutter fast. Screw each stem to a work-holding handle and, holding it obliquely, with the lines perpendicular, run it down the pencil lines, allowing the cutter to cut without force, and keeping it unwaveringly on the line. Cut all four to about half depth first, then finish to the full, remembering that it's easy to go too deep.

Rounded cutter

A round nose tool is used to scrape after pencilling so that progress is easily seen. Scrape the edges to round them, and paper to a smooth finish all round. The buff polishing will reveal parts that need more attention, but try not to burn! The neck is turned ⁷⁄₁₆ x ³⁄₄in diameter (11 x 19mm), and tapped ⁷⁄₃₂in (7mm) x 24.

Bishops' neck decoration and rounded cutter made from a nail

The top decoration is eight cuts with a vee cutter. The crests are then rounded with the same cutter, and a leaf decoration applied with a fine nail vee cutter. The bottom bead may also be incised with a few slanting scallops, using a rounded nail cutter. The mitre is connected to the neck with an ivory joining screw, and that completes our bishops.

Please note – or I may be in trouble! – none of this work bears the slightest resemblance to ornamental turning.

Chapter 16 ● *Chess Set:* Rooks *and* KNIGHTS

*I*n this chapter I want to concentrate on the rooks and knights. The rooks' stems are 2⅛in (54mm) long, plus the length of the screws, and are made in the same way as the other stems. The top is ²⁹⁄₃₂ x ²⁹⁄₃₂in (23 x 23mm).

The prepared ivory is held in the three jaw chuck by the top end, and the bottom bead and curve is turned, drilled and tapped ⁷⁄₃₂ x ¹⁵⁄₁₆in (6 x 24mm). It is then screwed onto an adapter chuck or plug, and the top is completed.

Rook components

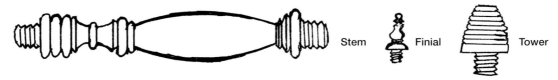

Stem   Finial   Tower

Top *Ivory patterns for the Pulpit chess set (1961), 4½in (115mm)*

ROOKS' CASTELLATIONS

The castellated part is recessed about ⅛in (3mm) deep, then drilled and tapped ¼ x ¹¹⁄₃₂in (6 x 26mm), to take the tower. To make the tower, turn the screw first and finish on an adapter plug in the three jaw. Tap a small hole in the top and make the finials to complete.

Using the same tiny drill we employed for the bishops' mitres (see page 102), drill eight holes around the castellated part, piercing the thin wall. With a vee cutter I made a pattern like the one shown below. A tiny vee cutter is used to make the brickwork, and this completes our rooks.

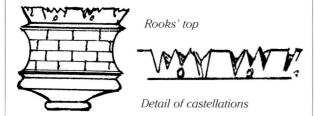

Rooks' top

Detail of castellations

KNIGHTS' STEMS AND NECKS

The knights were begun by turning the stems between centres, afterwards turning the threads at each end, using the same split boxwood collet I used on the pawns (see page 95).

The neck again was made on the adapter plug, like the bishops' necks, but I made eight grooves around the top with a small round cutter, and about a dozen oblique grooves at the bottom with a fine, rounded, nail cutter, each clamped in the three jaw.

We only need the horses heads to finish the whole set, but you must remember that the knight is the piece everyone looks at first, being the most animated and therefore the most interesting.

I know people who do not regard turning as a handcraft: they think of the lathe as a machine that does all the work while the operator just sticks a tool on it occasionally. The knight has to be fashioned by hand, and if it is a poor example, an otherwise good set is spoilt. On the other hand, if the knights are

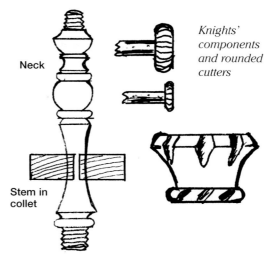

Neck

Stem in collet

Knights' components and rounded cutters

good, an otherwise poor set can very well pass. Take heart. My first knights were made for my very first chess set in 1950, in my own shop, over 100 miles from Bertram. They were 4½in (115mm) Stauntons.

I'm an ordinary craftsman, not a gifted artist, and those knights were on the crude side, but they were well finished and the set was bought by Alex Hammond, the chess afficionado. He knocked me down from £14 to £12 – the main reason I prefer to make work to order (once I'd escaped from the hawking and haggling brigade!). Hammond's set today would be worth not less than £500. With these notes and sketches, I expect you'll do better than I did all those years ago – I insist upon it.

I use the card from tea packets when I make templates for marking ivory when cutting. Whether you follow these sketches or have something else in mind, keep it simple. It's easy to set your sights too high.

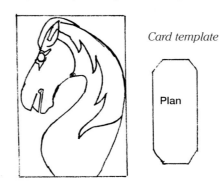

Card template

Plan

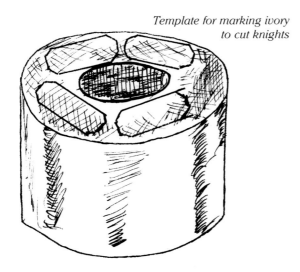

Template for marking ivory to cut knights

The small plan template is used to mark around the top of a suitable hollow section – or whatever is available. They are about 2in (50mm) high. I cut the blocks on my 6¹⁵⁄₁₆in (175mm) x 20SWG circular saw and trim the bottoms square. Next, I cut the head out of the card template with scissors, and use it to pencil the shape on each block. Sawing should result in something like that shown in the illustration below.

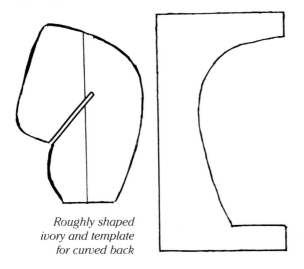

Roughly shaped ivory and template for curved back

The risky part is the oblique slot which, if wrongly placed, can leave insufficient room for the full mouth. Next, make a pencil line down the middle of the profile and mark the centre on the bottom. This will enable it to be

accurately fixed in the two or four jaw chuck, so the true axial line is assured as you drill about ½in (12mm) deep, and tap a thread ⁷⁄₁₆ x 24 teeth per inch. At the same time, taper turn the bottom, which ends in a circular section, to ⁹⁄₁₆in (14mm) diameter.

In the days before we learnt to cosset ourselves with two and four jaw chucks, I drilled and tapped them by hand, fixing drill and tap in a Jacobs chuck or three jaw.

A cardboard template will help to shape the back and trim the height to uniformity on the sanding disc. Pencil a line down the centre of the mane you've just sanded, from ears to base. You can check with a set square to ensure it is upright. The eye is pretty good at seeing if things are reasonably accurate, but when using carving cutters it's easy to go astray, as the piece is being moved in all directions, so the odd pencil line is a sound guide.

CARVING THE KNIGHTS' HEADS

Carving begins with the big cutter or hub, which roughs out the general shape. Cut the head width next, ¹⁷⁄₃₂in (13mm) at the top and ¹¹⁄₃₂in (9mm) at the mouth. I don't expect you to rough out the ears on this cutter because corners can easily be chipped off, but I hope you will get an idea of how far you can go on just this one large cutter from my sketches, right.

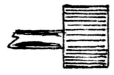

Cutter used for the ears

It is safer to cut in the ears with a nice little cutter like the one shown above. What we'll do next is mark the neck hole on both sides of each head in pencil, using the template. Drill a hole right through as large as you can risk, and then round out the neck shape as far as you can with a small conical cutter.

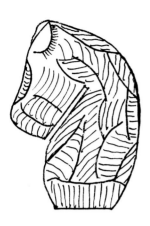

Views of the carving

I have a thin disc cutter, about ³⁄₃₂in (2mm), of 1¹⁵⁄₁₆in (48mm) diameter. Teeth are filed down on both sides. With this I remove the material between the chin and the chest – not completely, because finishing is done in the vice.

Conical cutter

I use the same cutter I used for the ears to run round the curve of the jaw and hollow the sides next to the mouth, which I have shaded in the sketch below. Make sure you get them all uniform.

Back to our conical cutter again, and get the underside of the jaw nicely rounded, using callipers to get them all alike. Cut in the curve under the neck, which I've arrowed in the sketch below. It's shaping nicely now.

Thin vee cutter for neck

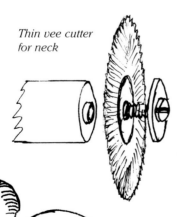

The curve under the neck needs to be cut in carefully

Hardwood clams are used in the leg vice to obviate bruising. They are sprung with a section of rubber hose, and chalk is applied where they grip. I fix the knight with the mouth facing upwards, and round the mouth with a strip of glasscloth, using it as the shoeshine boy used his polishing cloth. I also round the sloping top and the underside of the mouth.

It's easy to muck up the mouth so, at all stages, be sure you don't get the depth less than ½in (12mm). However, if anyone complains that the horses are not exactly alike, I tell 'em they can always get a much closer uniformity in moulded sets, but I am not in that business. Ours are guaranteed all different!

Here's a tricky little job I love – the railings (or teeth). Make an indent with a point tool exactly where shown in the sketch, above right, and drill right through with a ¹⁄₁₆in (1.5mm) spear drill. With the

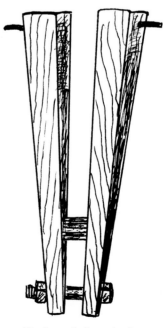

Hardwood clams in the vice will prevent bruising

A hole is drilled where the mouth ends

drill running in the lathe, you can look down on it as you drill and line it precisely by eye.

Before continuing, it's 'me dooty' to tell you again that all such craft is attended with risk so, if you prefer, just make a vee cut around the mouth. The result will be perfectly pleasing, but if you courageously elect to go on and chance it, you will have the thrill of hearing folk say, 'ooh, look at his teeth'. You need a fine slotting saw about ¹⁄₆₄ x 2in diameter (0.5 x 50mm). Sizes are purely academic, because in practice, we all use whatever we can lay hands on.

Set the tee rest thwartships and close to the left-hand side of the saw, the arbor of which is clamped in the three jaw, as the sketch below shows. Pencil a line around the mouth, ending at the bottom of the hole on each side. Hold the knight firmly in position upon the tee rest and make the slot which, you'll observe, is deliberately slanting to give the essential joviality to the horse.

A trickier operation follows – and it's too late now to change your mind about that simple

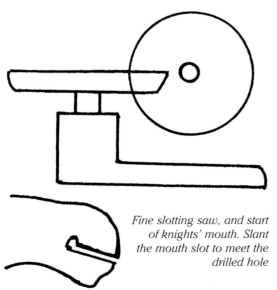

Fine slotting saw, and start of knights' mouth. Slant the mouth slot to meet the drilled hole

vee cut mouth. I'm afraid you'll have to make the cutter shown below, double size. Pencil a line around the mouth, ³⁄₃₂in (2mm) above the slot. The cutter is ³⁄₃₂in (2mm) thick. Fix the tee rest (parallel with the lathe bearers) 4in (100mm) or so away, as a support for your right hand on top, and your left hand below.

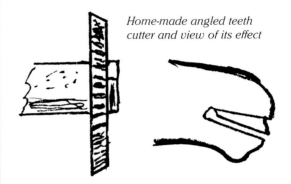

Home-made angled teeth cutter and view of its effect

Holding the knight head downwards, start the cutting on the left side hole, following that pencil line, as though your life depended on it, with the left side of the cutter, twisting the knight away from you and following the mouth evenly the whole way round.

Wow. It is tricky. I'll bet you're nervous! Don't be. Get a piece of round hardwood and have a little practice – a few minutes will give you confidence and you will then not spoil your work. If the cutter is well made, with about 18 teeth per inch, and you doggedly keep to that line, you will make a good job of it. Any fool can do easy work, but there's little joy in the easily attained.

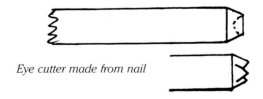

Eye cutter made from nail

The eyes have it. I'm afraid this is no push-over either, so you'll have to follow me to the letter. You will need a short rod of mild steel – a 3in (75mm) nail, beheaded, is perfect. Turn a taper on the end down to ⁹⁄₆₄in (3.5mm), and hollow out a nice hemisphere with a small round tool. Then, with a three square needle file, cut a few teeth round it while it's in the chuck – you'll only get about four. Try it on a piece of waste. It should cut a clean eye.

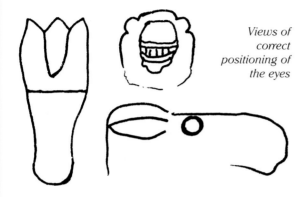

Views of correct positioning of the eyes

Preparation is important. I measured the head length – 1¼in (32mm), and put a pencil mark across half way. The part where the eyes come is about ½in (12mm) wide, but rounded so you'll be placing them at a slanting angle just below the top.

If your tee is set about 3in (75mm) away and at a 45° angle, it will support both hands as you press the precise part onto the eye cutter which is running at top speed.

Don't allow him to intimidate you – he'll buck you off if he can – but with lightness of touch, the proverbial iron hand in velvet glove, you will be victorious. Again, try a spot of practice first and get those eyes in the right places. If you don't quite succeed, lose no sleep over it, we'll allow it this once. I have never discarded a knight for the deviation of an eye.

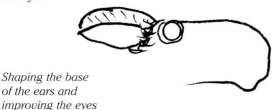

Shaping the base of the ears and improving the eyes

The next part is very rewarding. With the end section of the conical cutter, go around the eyes and shape the base of the ears, making an eyebrow, as I've tried to sketch below. It completes the structure of the ears and eyes convincingly. Next, put the point of that cutter half way along the sides of the ears and make a hollow in the pointed ends.

Now I pencil the line down the middle of the mane and, using one or more of my smooth cutters, go over the whole body, being careful not to let it snatch in the region of the ear points. I try to avoid making knights with perpendicular ears because I'm the bloke they come to for replacement ears when they've been hurled on the floor – as many chessmen are!

REMINISCING

Do you like the idea of spindle carving? The art of manipulating the workpiece around a fixed, revolving tool, instead of vice versa, is a knack which requires much getting used to. Once, long ago, I rigged a flexible drive with a cutter and, fixing the work in the vice, made my attack, hoping to find it much easier . . . Not a ha'p'th o' good. I could do nowt with it.

I need the firmness of a lathe to utilize cutters great and small, and after fiddling with that wretched scratching machine, I was heartily glad to get back to real carving – it really is a joy. I remember watching Bertram carving when I was a small boy and I never really wanted to do anything else but follow him. You could count the people in that trade, in London in the 1930s, on the fingers of two hands. I thought the 'old man' was a marvel and congratulated myself for my good fortune in having an ivory turner for a father. He'd been a turner/carver from a boy, as had his father and grandfather.

When he set up his own shop after the war, in 1919, most others had abandoned the trade. He told me how so many had said, 'this trade is finished'. 'But', said Bertram, 'I reckon if you can manage the variety of work, there ought to be enough trade to give you a living – and it's very pleasant, clean work.'

Bertram was always prepared to tackle jobs he hadn't done before. The old journeymen turners were not carvers, the carvers were not turners, so the combination of both gave a big advantage in setting up as a master.

> ## JOB satisfaction is the breath of life – to force a boy or girl into an office if the heart is elsewhere, is a fate worse than death

A particularly fine turner who worked for Holtzapffel for 40 years had a young son in the 1930s, who was so attracted to his father's wonderful lathe work that he began to practise on a Holtz lathe his father kept at home. When the turner realized where his son's heart lay he smashed the large flywheel. 'You, my boy,' he said, 'are going into an office.' And he jolly well did. The father had thought the trade was more or less finished.

Where Bertram differed in his outlook was in his contempt for schoolboard education. 'A college education,' he'd say, 'may get you a job – working for someone who hasn't had one!' He rescued me from school before I was 14 and I've had over 50 happy years turning in a trade that will never be finished because the lathe is the grand-daddy of all machine tools.

Job satisfaction is the breath of life – to force a boy or girl into an office if the heart is elsewhere, is a fate worse than death.

FILING AND SCRAPING

Enough of reminiscing. We're going to the clams now and we'll screw a rod into a knight as a holding piece in the jaws, while we go over the body with files and scrapers. The scraper is not only used on the body, but especially round the curves under the ears, and also on the tiny section between the eyes to the nose, not forgetting the tops of the ears which, otherwise, will appear rough when polished.

A narrow strip of glasscloth is capital for smoothing the neck and underside of the head. Don't forget to slide a piece into the saw-cut mouth and smooth upper and lower.

Take as much trouble with the mane as you wish. You may scrape the boundary so that the mane stands out, and vary the sizes of the vee cutters so that heavier vees separate different parts. You can also vary the direction and shape of the strokes effectively – and artistically. It is an unusual idea to have the two white knights with left hand mane, and opposite knights with right hand mane.

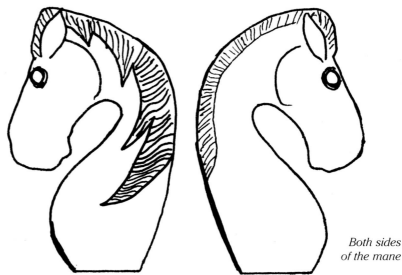

Both sides of the mane

DETAILING THE HEAD

We are not finished with the head yet. It is the facial scallops that impart character. One of the rounded cutters will achieve two broad ones each side of the head. The little cutter shown makes three smaller scallops running into the first two. The bottom one, done first, runs right into and blends with the lower lip. The three can be accommodated without running into the eye, but should this happen, go over the eye again with the eye cutter. Point in the nostrils with a small drill – convincingly – but don't overdo this. You may also point in the teeth.

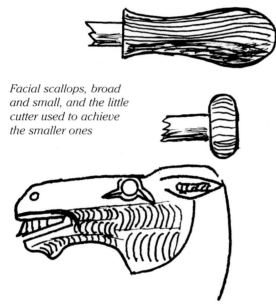

Facial scallops, broad and small, and the little cutter used to achieve the smaller ones

The last job, the eye corners, is with your best little vee cutter – take care not to let it run into the eyeballs – and the crafty line all round the upper lip, ending in downward sweeps like Fu Manchu's moustache. Pencil it first, and concentrate.

When you buff polish, do not force the buff to remove scratches and blemishes, but pencil over the offending parts and scrape them clear in the clams before buffing again.

When all is done, a soak in hot water and brushing with a toothbrush will complete, and

I hope you'll be as pleased with the result as I am. The joining screws are now made, and that is the final job on the lathe.

STAINING

For staining, I'm using a vegetable dye made up for me which achieves the lovely colour of horse chestnuts. First immerse the pieces in hot water with lemon washing-up liquid, then brush thoroughly with old toothbrushes and rinse in warm water.

On the stove, your stainless steel or enamel saucepan of dye is hot, but not too hot to touch. Pour in a tablespoonful of acetic acid – or non-brewed condiment that passes for vinegar – which acts as a mordant. Put all the pieces in the dye and keep them moving with a stick of wood until the colour reaches the depth required.

With a lid over the top, pour the dye into another container and then put the pieces straight into a bowl of clean, hot water. Brush each one with a soft brush and set them out to dry – not less than six hours.

They are then glossed on a swansdown buff with a glossing compo such as fine white porthos. My buff is an old one I keep for reds, worn down to 4in (100mm). My knights came up beautifully.

KEEP it simple! It's easy to set your sights too high

A final thought. We craftsmen are the whipping boys today, whether 'tis rainforest hardwoods, ivory or whatever. We've been doing our jobs for thousands of years and haven't changed, so pardon us if we refuse to feel guilty. When the gangsters, vandals, poachers and ruiners of this beautiful earth are liquidated, we'll still carry on – and the earth will recover.

Chapter 17 ● *Adapting* IDEAS *and* DESIGNS

As an avid reader of literature I'm forced to the conclusion that I'm a rotten writer. Yet I take comfort in the fact that hardly anything in the world is original. When a great writer said to a friend – after they'd just heard a gem of wit – 'I wish I had said that,' the friend retorted (and I don't believe a word of it myself), 'You will Oscar – you will!'.

I say why not! Of what use is the gift of writing if not to share good things? Plagiarism it is not. Tom Lehrer rightly called it research. Why shouldn't we make a virtue out of necessity and say, with Montaigne, 'I string together other people's posies, but the thread that binds them is my own'.

The best of writers all use the posies of others and often their own thread may well outshine them. Original geniuses are rare, but nearly everyone who wishes can shine at whatever the mind turns to, using the experience of others to support their own.

There is no shame in adapting the ideas and examples of others – especially if we give them the credit. Nothing is completely new. For example, there are only two kinds of painters (artists) – those who paint from photographs and those who admit they do.

Really, I suppose, from a mere handful of master craftsmen and artists, have descended myriads of others producing works equally good as any of the past. Unfortunately though, it does help to sell an artist's work if he or she happens to have been dead for several centuries!

> ORIGINAL geniuses
> are rare, but nearly
> everyone who wishes
> can shine at whatever
> the mind turns to, using
> the experience of others
> to support their own

What a colossal sham this world is! The only way to enjoy it without bitterness is to be oblivious to fame and fortune – the greatest sham o' the lot! Remember, however much we emulate or borrow from others, each one of us is unique, and the advice I find most apposite comes from Andre Gide:

'What another would have done as well as you do, do not do it. What another would have said as well as you do, do not say it; written as

113

Left *Polyester resin salt mill with ivory key, 3in (75mm) – chiefly handwork and very precise* well, do not write it. Be faithful to that which exists nowhere but in yourself – and thus make yourself indispensable.'

Gide (pronounced Zheed) has also resolved my problem on the best subjects to choose when 'penning my stunners', as squire Surtees might have said. I shall stick to my own experiences and enjoy it. There is only one B. J. (thankfully). Irreplaceable? Very! But indispensable? I'm working on it – aren't we all?

A DYING TRADE

In the early 1950s, when I had begun to stop worrying about having enough work to keep me solvent, another one of my 'old characters' stepped into my turning shop. He was an ordinary looking little man in his seventies. His name was Phesay, and his life had been spent turning ivory collar studs – front, back, dress, some with gold and mother-of-pearl. He claimed they'd last a lifetime – if you didn't lose 'em!

Sez he, 'I'm retiring soon and moving down to live with my daughter in Worthing. My father was in this business, and it has always kept me – in fact I've bought a house out of it. I know that when I pack up, this trade will too,' he continued, 'because there's no-one left to carry on. I wondered if you might like to take it over. I have some lathes and gear which you could have for a song – and I'd pass my clients to you. What d'you say?'

'Well,' I said, 'I should think it would be possible. How much do you get for ivory studs?'

'I used to get fourpence each, but now it's sixpence. You get your ivory from waste which you can buy for next to nothing. I'll show you exactly how to go about it.'

Now before anyone sneers at one-sixtieth of a quid, remember you could buy a fish and chip dinner and get a penny change in the times he was talking about, so think on . . .

I explained to the dear old soul, gently, that at present I had about enough to do and that sixpence (one-fortieth of a pound) for an ivory stud was less than half the value I considered necessary to make them a proposition. And, appreciating my viewpoint, after a few more words, he left.

I spoke to old Louis, a famous ivory man, about Phesay, and Louis said, 'That house was left to him in a legacy – he didn't buy it out of the profits from studs! He can make it pay because he's never made anything else and has hardly any overheads.'

I had completely forgotten Phesay when, one year later, in he walked again.

> # THERE is no shame in adapting the ideas and examples of others – especially if we give them the credit

'I thought over what you said and I upped the price to eightpence. I believe, if I passed my best clients over to you, they'd agree to tenpence each,' he said. 'Would you be interested at that? Only it's a shame to allow a good line to become extinct.'

'All right, I'll have a go!' I agreed, and arranged to visit him at St Ann's Road, Tottenham, where he had a room as a workshop with a couple of treadle lathes. There, he showed me his methods from start to finish, the waste ivory he bought, and the quality of work expected. Some of the studs were half bark and not very good, but at his prices I wasn't surprised.

'I'll let you know when I'm ready to go,' he said.

TAKING OVER

A month later he looked in.

'I'm off to Worthing next week. If you will call at my shop, I've left the bits and bobs you might find useful. Just give the housekeeper whatever you consider they're worth to you.

The Rescue

What's this? A poor old lathe head lying under lumber in the rain.
Well old warrior, I don't need you I'm afraid,
Lie there a little longer-friend, and by and by
Some kindly lumber-man may set you on the road
To steel-land where the hungry furnace
Will free your aching limbs and make you young again.

For what? Aye, there's a thought! Whatever you'll become,
Its pounds to pancakes you'll be a paltry thing beside a lathe,
Perhaps you'll can some beans or help some monumental ass to shave!
But this is morbid talk — I'd help you if I could
But damn it! I've got Stamford hill to climb

With heavy sacks of ivory waste athwart my bike...
I'll wager your old master, now retired,
Or mayhap his father — who can tell?
Bought you in some junk shop for a song
And set you up to earn his crusts making studs.
Nothing else! by day, by night, by treadle and by gaslight.

And yet he didn't quite desert it all,
Some afterthought had made him send me word
That what he'd left was mine and with it his
Best trade in studs to supplement my work,
I have my load prepared, the lathe alone remains.
I shall no more return — and yet I stay
To contemplate the rust that even now
Begins to wrap you up as in a shroud...

My turning shop at last, I made it, ask not how,
The gear unloaded, packed away and now
For you my beauty, well, I vow
You guessed I'd never leave you in that plight,
I liked your line — your mandrel's rusted firm,
But firm it is and that's a healthy sign.
Now your quite dismantled, all the rust is gone,
Your tapered steel front bearing is still good
Your tail pin on the skew, I'll get it true
With whirling stone obliquely in the slide rest set.

Your first run-in was not a huge success,
You'd never please the real perfectionist!
But what dull expert knows the master's touch,
The trained encouragement to cull
A real performance from the likes of you?
The hours of patient coaxing & the work-inspiring force
Which scatters defects and charms perfection
From a bygone dream.

Your happy turning days begin anew
And those who love to turn
And credit sentient feelings to a thing of steel
Will joy with me that you can run again.

There's a quantity of ivory pieces, a lathe and a few useful tools. She'll be glad of anything. Here's a list of clients. I have notified the two best ones that they can get studs from you, but here's my new address, and please drop me a line, as I'd like to know how you get on. I'll help you if you run into trouble. Don't let the old trade die out lad, even if you only do a few now and then.' He really was a dear old chap wasn't he.

Next day I rode on my bike from DeBeauvoir Town to Tottenham – about 7 miles (4.5km) – and called in. The housekeeper, Mrs Gunn, took me through to the garden where I was glad to see there was little of interest to me. His tools had been mainly old files, and he had taken a lathe and some gear, possibly to use at Worthing. Even the files were worn down to a couple of inches. There was a sack or two of ivory, mostly rubbish – and a headstock. That's all! I wrote down what happened in blank verse.

THE PHESAY METHOD

Now, old Phesay used any ivory pieces that would yield a collar stud – end or plank grain went in. He marked the requisite circle on the base in pencil, and cut round it as closely as possible on his 6in (150mm) circular saw, which screwed onto the mandrel, for attic-masters seldom had space for a separate sawbench.

Straight from the saw, the blanks were pressed into a boxwood spring chuck and the iron ring was banged on to tighten. He then turned the stem, but left the head unfinished so that he could reverse it in another spring chuck to finish the back. Reversing it again in a third spring chuck, he completed the turning and gave it the first polish in the lathe, with compo and a piece of felt. It was finally polished beautifully on the buff. The simple tools, round, straight, point and screever (for

115

parting) were all made from three square files, which are superior for such work to any manufactured ones.

For perfection of tooling, the hardwood and ivory turner would prefer to have the best cutting finish and keep renewing the edge, rather than sacrifice something of that perfection just to cut down on the sharpening.

FILES were used because they were convenient and good, not to avoid buying manufactured tools

Files were used because they were convenient and good, not to avoid buying manufactured tools, which were quite cheap in those days. Remember, they've gone up 150 times! Your one and tenpenny chaser is now 15 quid!

Every turner finds his or her own ways of working, but I decided to begin by copying the master first, so I made a number of boxwood spring chucks. You can't have too many to accommodate the small variations in sizes and to allow for wear, which is considerable when chucking rough sawn pieces.

After putting up with this nonsense for a gross or so, an old saw came to my aid, viz,

'Why be difficult when, with a little more effort, you can be well nigh impossible!', for this method was so hard on the boxwood, that I was refurbishing the chuck too time-wastingly often. So – I chucked it!

THE JONES METHOD
In a week I devised the Jones method, which works as follows:

1 Mark out the stud ivory using templates with the requisite diameters for front and back studs.

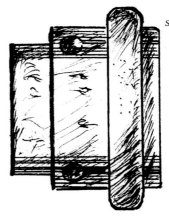

Brass and steel spring chuck with stopping piece

2 Saw them as close as possible on my little circular saw.
3 Grip them in the three jaw so that the pencilled circle runs truly, and turn slightly tapered to fit a cup chuck. (This chuck is a

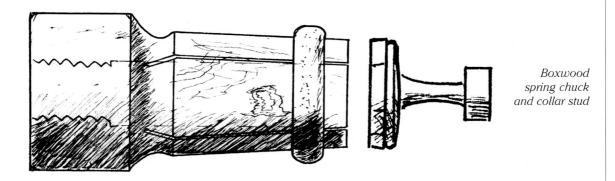

Boxwood spring chuck and collar stud

beauty – a Holtzapffel brass spring chuck, stopped with a nicely turned piece of tough and durable whale tooth. The hole is accurately opened, almost, but not quite straight-sided. When turning the blanks to fit, they must enter only $\frac{1}{16}$in (1.5mm). With my foot-controlled lathe I could prepare three blanks a minute.)

4 Complete all but the backing off in the first turning.

5 Turn the backs in a spring collet in the three jaw. The front studs, being longer than backs, pass through an ivory stepped washer first. (The horn collet, of smaller diameter than the back of a stud, is bored right through, the hole being about two-thirds the diameter of the top of the stud.)

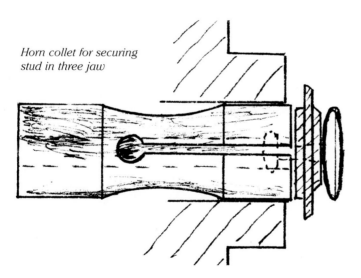

Horn collet for securing stud in three jaw

Three slots are sawn half way, terminating in holes drilled through the side. A hollow or cove is turned where the holes are situated, and when the stud is pressed in and the collet gripped in the three jaw, it is firmly and safely held and based off in a trice with the square tool and armrest (you know my methods). These collets last indefinitely, as most good, natural materials do, and are trouble free, if the right turner uses 'em!

For back studs, I simply replace the whale stopper with another, opened to a larger diameter, and when backing off, I eliminate the ivory washer.

I quickly became adept at the job, which I enjoyed immensely on my Holtz Vampire lathe, and brought them up to a very fair price of one and tuppence each. They constituted half my trade for some years, and I knocked up three gross a week when engaged upon them, usually to the accompaniment of Scottish or Irish dance music, which is a surefire way of keeping you from being overcome by monotony.

I always tried to make each stud better than the last. Only beautifully sharpened files were used. Half the polishing was done in the chuck by the application of a small chunk of Cannings Crown tripoli compo and a piece of felt. The finishing was done on the buff, but they really fly when you least expect it!

Until fairly recently, I still did the odd gross or two at a greatly advanced price, and often thought of others in this world with a weight of worry on their shoulders, pondering over complications and botherations of all kinds – working their poor old brains to the bone. And there was I, quietly tapping pieces of ivory into bits of whale with a 1½lb (680kg) ball pein hammer, and effortlessly and impeccably turning collar studs on an 1813 Holtzapffel & Deyerlein lathe that runs like a Spinning Jenny.

I appreciate that it's not everyone's cup o' tea, but I wouldn't willingly change places with anyone in this world. I know old Phesay would be pleased too.

Chapter 18
Alternative Turning
MATERIALS

T he turning shop is like a flour mill this morning, except that the dust is red along with the white. I've just finished two sets of 'Jaques' Staunton chessmen, with 4½in (115mm) kings made from polyester resin (alternative ivory). I marvel to think that in 1950 I got £12 for a set made in solid ivory and now these sets from man-made ticky-tacky will fetch 30 times that much – an unbelievable change in the value of money.

Above Cutting barleycorns with the balanced eccentric cutting frame on the Eldorado lathe

POLYESTER RESIN

I'll tell you a horror story about ticky-tacky, straight and unvarnished from my shop's log. 'Friday, 11 May 1990: not a good day, damp and dull. (I always start with a weather report.) I'm up at six to get an hour in before breaker. Turning away at the king tops, I find all the shavings at my feet blazing.'

Polyester resin shavings are much finer than casein and infinitely more inflammable, as I found out! A frond had ignited on the one-bar electric fire and the flame ran along it like a fuse, firing the mass at my feet. It did no good to stamp on the fire – it was too extensive and getting a firmer hold by the second, while the blackest of thick, choking smoke began to fill the workshop.

> ## POLYESTER resin shavings are much finer than casein and infinitely more inflammable, as I found out!

I tried to smother it with a heavy blanket, but even this did not stop it. Flames were everywhere. I rushed to unship my fire extinguisher, bought 40 years ago, the kind you aim and fire like a gun. I pulled back the cocking lever, but it was loose and I could get no sense out of it. I was choking and blinded as, desperately, I rushed outside for air, but outside the doors was a large mound of wet grass cuttings which, fortuitously, I cut only yesterday. Seizing a double armful, I walked back to the fire and smothered all the front flames.

There was enough grass to take handfuls from the top and put paid to those flames under the bench. I opened the windows then rushed out for air.

After ensuring the fire was really out, I nipped indoors, away from the smoke, and watched from the kitchen window to check it really was abating. Suddenly I glimpsed my face in the mirror. I looked like Al blooming Jolson! Fresh waves of smoke started issuing from the shop, so I galloped back with a wet handkerchief over my nose, as the atmosphere was literally lethal.

Inside I found the sack I had thrown away as ineffective blazing merrily and setting fire to a wooden box. I soon whipped that outside and smothered it with wet grass. Even then it continued to smoulder and smoke until I fetched a watering can to it.

After a shower and a change, when the smoke had dispersed, I had a good clear up. I thought of the salutary lessons to be observed. Such a happening would be far less likely with good old natural materials. Also with casein which, based on milk, would not have spread like wildfire, quicker than I could stamp it out. Quite evidently, I must not allow shavings to accumulate, but clear them frequently.

Further, a closed-in heater is preferable. Also of paramount importance is a tip in *Awake* magazine which my daughter drew to my attention – causing both of us to fall about laughing. It had been an article which read: 'Those responsible for safety should know where all the fire extinguishers are and how to use them. It is too late to read the instructions after the fire breaks out.' I can vouch for that. You can't read 'em for black smoke.

Of course, after the fire I discovered I had failed to pull back the hammer until it clicked. Is the material safe? Yes, in the solid it's as safe as most things, but in fine shavings it must be respected, and by clearing bench and floor frequently it will be safe. That was the end of turning for that day. It was many days ere the stench left the workshop.

Three days later I wrote this in the log: 'I continued with the queens – my word. This material gets no easier to turn and I sigh with anguish and despair at the loss of ivory, which is so easy by comparison.' Yet after work was completed, it really looked so good that all the snags were forgotten. If this is what we we're left with, I'm going to make the best of it.

ALTERNATIVE IVORY

An increasing number of craftsmen are making works of art from alternative ivory and, surely, a fine piece of work must not be under-valued simply because of the material which is, in the main, indistinguishable from ivory, and, of course, is much cheaper.

I have to convince myself this is not cheap plastic (at £15 a kilo (2.2lb) I should say not), it really is alternative ivory. I'll use it like ivory too. It is non-toxic and, when sawn, although the dust is affectionate (clinging) it has no unpleasant or chemical smell. In fact, it is quite a friendly material. It will not stand the heavy-handed approach and would splinter like the Dickens under a gouge. A sharp round tool, gently applied well below centre height, will produce all the shavings you want – that's how one of them reached the electric fire.

If some gets spoiled it's no tragedy – there's plenty of it. It doesn't crack and it isn't defective. It's a pretty handy shape when all is considered, and if it is not ivory it jolly well looks like it and may have to be our ivory from now on. When I carved the knights I found no problems. The stuff likes my carving cutters, evidently, and that's an important point in its favour.

LEMONWOOD

Let's try something else. Wood. I've been turning some lovely organ draw stop knobs out of lemonwood. It is close-grained, but not so hard as the superior boxwood. It has less character too, but quite nice withal.

The square lengths are supplied to me cut and I'm left with enders about 1–1⅜ x 1⅜in diameter (25–35 x 35mm). I have a few score of these

pieces and loads of the same in rosewood. I cannot think (at the moment) of anything better to use such stock for than little boxes.

I remember the Reverend Standish Ensell, who wrote a marvellous article in Bulletin No. 3 of the Society of Ornamental Turners (around 1950), entitled 'My Lathes'. Here's how he began:

'When I was a small boy of about seven or eight years of age, I was wandering one day about the village in which we lived (about 1875) and I chanced to meet the rector, who was a friend of my father.

'He came up to me and, I think I was looking rather desolate and forlorn, said "Come and

Holtzapffel ornamental lathe with overhead gear

have some tea and I will show you my lathe". That's got to be the finest invitation in the English language, and that was the first time I ever saw an ornamental lathe.

'My kind host got a bit of olive wood and turned a delightful little box and lid. Then he produced a tool that was driven by a band from a contraption above the lathe, and before my astonished eyes, cut a beautiful pattern.

'He told me the tool was made by a man with, to me, an unpronounceable name (many years were to pass before I could spell it) and he told me it had cost the, to me, immense sum of £9 19s. 0d.

'The whole scene is as vivid before my eyes as it if happened yesterday. The neat little white tie, the immaculate clothes (even the clergy could afford to dress decently in those days), the kind face and the clever hands – and that is 74 or 75 years ago.'

I've never forgotten that article, and many's the time I have turned a boxwood box for a visitor, inlaid the lid with ivory and decorated it with the eccentric cutting frame. 'Wonderful,' they all say, and of course I reply, 'Elementary, my dear Watson.' (I really do.)

THREAD CHASING

Now the idea of using lemonwood is a challenge, because it isn't noted for standing up to thread chasing like boxwood, nor is it suitable for ornamental turning. Still, I thought, I don't know for sure that such woods are unsuitable. The people who affirmed such things were stocked up with choice ivory and the finest woods recommended for ornamental turning work, so they didn't even bother to try. Maybe extra care and determination might succeed – it's worth a shot. I had a go by making half a dozen. Here's how.

First, turn matching male and female threads on something hard. I used polyester resin, but blackwood or box will serve. These are used to get the box threads uniform, so that finishing

and decoration can be done by screwing lid and body to these pieces, which are held in the three jaw chuck. The hard patterns are necessary because the softer lemonwood bruises badly in self-centring chucks.

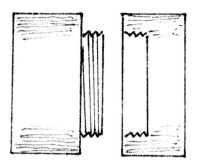

Hardwood pattern for male and female threads

As lemonwood tends to crumble in normal chasing, I said extra care might succeed, so chasers must be sharp and applied with more than the usual delicacy. In the customary manner, the tee rest is parallel with, and about ¾in (20mm) away from the work, and slightly below centre height. The fingers of the left hand are all below the tee and around the pedestal, the left thumb on top of the chaser which is in position for business, but instead of the right hand holding the chaser handle by the end, it is close by the left hand, merely giving support to the chaser.

Striking is as usual, the teeth being gently moved by the right hand to describe a series of clockwise circles close to the work and below centre height.

With the lathe speed about 200rpm, strike the thread when the tool is moving to the left, at the bottom of its circular movement, using the middle of the chaser on the slightly rounded corner of the work.

It is a dragging cut, as you can see, and the only pressure comes from the weight of the handle. The right hand guides without the slightest pressure. All right, so your lowest lathe speed is 400rpm, you move the chaser a little faster – it's all a matter of what one gets used to.

121

Failure to cut threads is often the result of directing the chaser as an ordinary turning tool – the chaser has a mind of its own and refuses to be directed. If you push it at the wrong rate of traverse or stop its movement for a second, it will play the cat and banjo with you: you move it in the right direction, at a rate of traverse you will learn by trial and error.

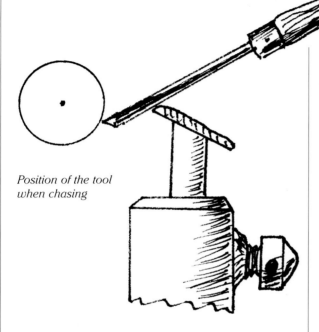

Position of the tool when chasing

With absolutely no pressure, simply allow it to cut its own thread. You never stop the chaser, at any short traverse, because it will immediately cut a series of unscrew-like rings. You simply make the traverse and remove it from the cut to begin again, at the rate of about one per second.

Always keep this in mind as you practise: 'On the plains of hesitation bleach the bones of millions who, at the dawn of victory, sat down to rest, and, resting, died.' So don't give up – victory is nearer than you think.

Hopefully the sharp teeth will remove the wood painlessly, as you almost will it not to crumble. As the thread deepens, turn the crests down a trifle with a flat tool, until you have the size you want.

CRUMBLING

A slightly flattened crest is also advisable for the finished thread, to discourage any crumbling. Should the thread crumble a little, be sure to make a virtue out of necessity. Many modern woodturners now are using old and imperfect chunks of timber with natural edges and sundry orifices in all directions, which would have been consigned to the waste box not too long ago.

I don't want to hear any of those guys criticizing my crumbling threads. I make 'em crumble – artistically of course. But it's great fun!

The same gentle manipulation is necessary when cutting the inside threads, using an armrest. The inside one on the lid is turned first, then fitted to the body. Having cut the thread on the body, I hollow it out nicely, then smooth and polish it inside with wax applied on 0000 grade steel wool.

A FINE piece of work must not be under-valued simply because of the material

At present I'm using Goddard's cabinet maker's wax polish, which I bought years ago, as it had such a fine Chippendale picture on the tin. It is also delightfully lavender-scented. Don't apply it on cloth, which can be dangerous. Kitchen roll is good enough for my friend and mentor Chris Stott, and it's good enough for me.

I wax the threads at the same time so that the lid fits well, neither too tight nor too loose. Screw the lid on firmly, but gently, having regard to the soft nature of the wood, and turn the whole to any shape you fancy.

The base is turned by screwing the body into the female pattern held in the three jaw. Here I must give another friend and mentor, Bonnie Klein, a mench, because she has suggested that the application of superglue to wood about to be threaded, has a strengthening and crumble-discouraging effect, and I'm all in favour.

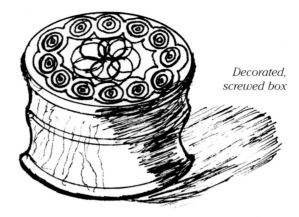

Decorated, screwed box

changes ad infinitum.

As I thought, the cuts appear lighter on the polished surface and, of course, they do not sparkle like the eyes of an ornamental turner

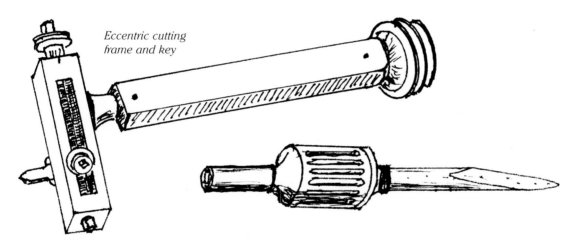

Eccentric cutting frame and key

ECCENTRIC

We've proved that reasonable threads can be executed on softer woods, now we'll try decorating the lid with the eccentric cutting frame. No abrasives are used on parts to be ornamented, but polish the whole box first. I do mine on the calico buff with Cannings Crown compo.

In the eccentric cutting frame, I fit a double-angle point tool with a 50° angle 'well got up', i.e., sharpened on an Arkansas stone to make various patterns, including interlacing circles – nothing to strain the brain. Between 5 and 10 minutes is ample, and you can ring the

who has just cut a lustrous pattern on ivory, but let us try the wax polish again, applied with a soft brush. I've always got a few old tooth-brushes for every occasion – and even fewer old teeth, I'm afraid! The patterns came up very much better than I expected, and I must vote the whole enterprise a total success.

My conclusions are that when we had all the ivory we wanted we could denigrate lesser materials as being unacceptable for ornamental turning: now, 'all is grist', and whatever comes to hand can possibly be utilized and ornamentally turned. Maybe we'll be seeing some surprises on the show tables . . .

Chapter 19 ● *The* Puzzle BALL *and the* Magic HAMMER

S aturday, 25 September 1993: I paid a visit to London's Camden Passage, a hotbed of antiques on Saturdays. It is easy to reach; simply alight at the Angel (on the Northern Line). One of the longest escalators in London will bring you to the surface, when you simply ask the first convenient person to point you in the direction of Camden Passage, a few hundred paces along the road.

I went to see a chess afficionado, Donald Goddard, in his shop which I thought was called Donay & Teakes – my hearing is notoriously unreliable! It turned out to be Donay

Above Ivory rattle made using rose and vertical cutting frames – chiefly handwork

124

Antiques. I had a lovely day, enhanced by a delightful pub lunch. I told Donald I came here regularly in the 1930s, to Levy's, a fine gramophone shop. When I walked in my good friend the proprieter would say, 'Ah! I'm glad you've come – I've got just the record for you,' and on his super-duper radiogram, vastly superior to the machines of today, he'd reverently place something he knew I couldn't resist, say Peter Dawson singing The Old Superb or Young Tom o' Devon, and thrill me to the marrow.

'I don't think I can afford both this week,' I'd say. 'Ho!' sez he, 'If you wait till you can afford things you'll never get them.' Usually I did. I've still got most of those records, and sometimes play them when I'm working. What a treat. They don't play 'em on Classic FM.

Donald said, 'Now I'll tell you something – mine is the very shop that used to be Levy's.' What a coincidence. He still has a few of the tiny HMV gramophone needle tins as a memento. His main stock in trade are Staunton chessmen and ancient games, many and various.

Three puzzle balls

It was a most rewarding day both for business and interest, as my attention was drawn to a small curio new to me, though evidently old in origin. It was handed to me as a friendly challenge and looked a whit formidable, although it was but a simple wooden ball concealing a box.

I was non-committal because I never feel overconfident until I've had a go. As a puzzle, it was no rival to the Rubik cube (which has been likened to the Gordian Knot, requiring not a knife, but a 9lb (4kg) lump hammer).

I WAS non-committal because I never feel overconfident until I've had a go

The ball was a friendly thing to handle, with six symmetrically spaced groups of eight concentric rings, with a dimple in the centre of each group arranged like the faces of a die, except that it's a sphere, not a cube. When the correct dimple is pressed, it ejects a lidded box, the lid being the ringed portion opposite the dimple. How simple – yet I wondered if the accurate placing of the six positions might require delving into the inscrutable realms of higher mathematics, in which case I'd give up for a start.

TURNING THE BALL

Back in my turning shop, however, I found, on inspection, that the groups were not spaced dead accurately, the ancient turner having an eye on production in the time-honoured way of the days when turners had to work and not fool about with non-essentials.

Selecting a piece of alternative ivory rod (polyester resin), approximately the same diameter, I turned a ball. The easiest way to do this is by making a template, by turning a ring with a hole a whisker bigger than the diameter of the required ball, and cutting the ring into two semicircles. This gives you one template and a spare, which almost immediately loses itself.

With good tools used upon the armrest, a perfect sphere is speedily achieved, except for the end where you cut it off and which has to be finished, with the help of the template, by reversing in the three jaw. This, of course, will not give billiard ball accuracy, but certainly a ball that the unaided eye will pass as near enough: but we are not ready to cut it off yet.

THE RINGS

The outside ring diameter for all six groups is such that there should be a small margin separating it from each of its four neighbours. This is arrived at by trial, error, and 'an ordinary lead pencil' (as Kenneth and George used to boast). So long as it's not oversize, the exact gap is decidedly non-critical. The next essential is to make a first series of rings.

Having circled a pencil line at the exact diameter on which I'd determined, I used a 16 outside chaser, and placing the left hand tooth on the line, with the tool sloping down below centre height to avoid any catches, I cut the tiny vee. I did this gradually moving the handle round, following the curve until the rings were all cut, leaving about ¼in (6mm) plain at the centre. In the absence of such a chaser simply make the necessary vee cuts with a flat point tool or, alternatively, make a suitable form tool from a flat piece of steel, by filing the teeth with a triangular needle file.

A number 16 hand chaser

The next step is to bore a hole about ¼in (6mm), right through the ball, making sure it's accurate by using the armrest. Then I part off the ball.

Position of the first three concentric circles

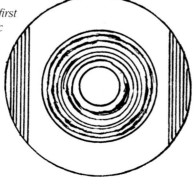

Not having to worry about bruising with polyester, I reversed it in the three jaw, centring the drill hole exactly. Then, using the template, I completed the sphere, marked the outer ring in pencil, same as the first, and turned another set of eight rings.

Loosening the chuck, I swivelled the ball 90° and made a trial circle with pencil. With a little adjustment I got the circle exactly midway between the two sets, marked the correct diameter and turned the third group.

We have to reverse it again, and to ensure accuracy, mark a pencil line on the equator so it will guide us in getting the fourth set dead right.

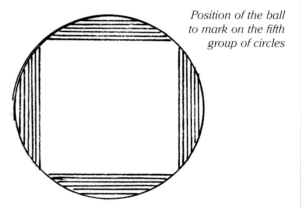

Position of the ball to mark on the fifth group of circles

As you see, so far we've spaced four groups without any mathematical calculations. The last two couldn't be simpler. Swivel 90° again and we have a blank space with four groups surrounding it. Adjust the ball until your trial pencilled circle is dead centre, equi-distant from each group. Turn the rings, finishing with a shallow dimple in the middle. I didn't dimple the first two, which were bored, but the rest I did. Reverse the ball and make the last group similarly accurately.

OPENING THE HOLE

Now I return the ball to its original position, where I first drilled it, and with inside tools I open a wide, slightly tapered hole as per sketch.

The width of the top is the same as the second ring of the group. I didn't measure the

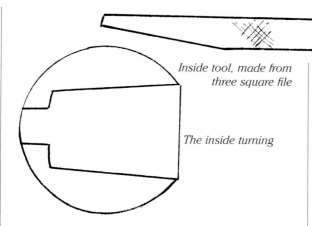

Inside tool, made from three square file

The inside turning

angle of the taper, but if it is too straight, the box may jam in too tightly to be removed without force. The bottom taper, of much smaller diameter, can be turned now by first enlarging the hole to about ¼in (6mm), then tapering it with a narrow inside tool. The tapered parts are then papered and wax polished by lapping the paper etc. around a thin rod.

FITTING THE BOX

Now for the box, which is simply turned to fit inside the ball perfectly. It cannot be rushed – you must take as long as you need because it is precision work without a mike.

As it approaches the finish, the ball is pressed on gently, but firmly, and removed, when you will observe exactly where the high spots are by the portions that shine.

Keep removing the high spots very gently until the box beds home. Remember you have both tapers to fit equally exactly. Don't make a sloppy fit – it needs to bed fully home without any play, and with the bottom end protruding ⅛ or 5⁄32in (3 or 4mm). Then, with the ball jammed well home, turn the bottom stub and finish with a dimple like the others. Take off the ball and cut off the box ⅛in (3mm) from the top.

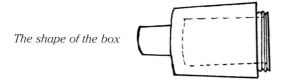

The shape of the box

Secure the box in the three jaw, protecting it with a double thickness of abrasive paper. I turned down a shoulder and cut thereon a 24 thread, hollowed it out, carefully measuring the depth, then sanded and waxed the interior and the threads. The puzzle box I had as a pattern had a push fit lid and you may prefer to do the same. The lid finishes the puzzle. Just fit the box to it.

As usual, I made a fancy pattern inside with a small, flat, point tool and a ⅛in (3mm) round nose, not forgetting to wax finish nicely. It's always the finishing touches that mark the work of a master: it's not always the skill – it's the extra care.

The ball is then tried on and the lid turned to slide into it, not too tightly, but tight enough for the join to be hidden when finished.

Interior of lid

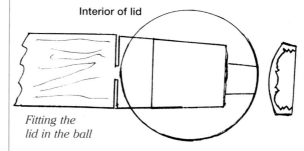

Fitting the lid in the ball

With the ball pressed home, the lid is parted off, following the contour of the sphere with room for finishing. I then fixed it truly in the three jaw and completed the turning, using the template, turned the eight rings and dimple, then polished the whole on the calico mop with Cannings Crown compo.

DEMONSTRATION

It had taken an hour and I rather liked it as a project, as I felt it could be popular and attractive. I therefore occupied a day making several of them in some boxwood I've had for 30 years; certainly well seasoned.

I had a demo session coming up, with the Thameside Woodturning Association at Leigh-on-Sea, and wondered whether I could perfect my act for the occasion. I decided to risk it for the following reasons: it would be a complete change from the norm; it would entail risk and that always enlivens the proceedings; and further, as a new project, many might care to try making them themselves.

I always use cup chucks for boxwood, but at present I have none which fit the lathes I'm given for demos. I have therefore made a brass arbor which I clamp in a three or four jaw chuck. On this I screw my brass cup chuck.

Brass arbor for holding chucks in three or four jaw

This seemingly perfect solution to the problem is not perfect because every extension you make between mandrel nose and chuck reduces rigidity so that the turning ease and facility is reduced by about 25%. I shall, I think, find out the particulars of the various mandrel nose sizes in future, so that I can make my own cup chucks to fit.

About 50-odd rolled up to see me. 'You've been honoured tonight,' said one, 'There's a World Cup match on.' Phew! Everyone seemed to enjoy the project, which went exceedingly well. I banged the prepared boxwood – well-chalked for a good grip – firmly into the chuck with my 1½lb (680kg) ball pein hammer, and turned the ball.

When I'd drilled it through, I measured and marked for the outside ring and cut them with the 16 chaser. Leaving only the outside one on its own, I hollowed out the interior and made the two tapers, large and small, and wax finished the inside. Then, I cut the ball off, and opened out the piece of wood left in the chuck to a nice, slight taper that fitted the ball to perfection (a job you mustn't hurry).

MAGIC HAMMER

All I had to do was tap that ball into the chuck so that the small hole was running dead true. I used two friends to ensure this; my piece of Canvey chalk (without which it won't grip), and my non-bruising, special, home-made boxwood hammer. This is used with some care in a series of taps, culminating in the *coup de grâce* when a heavier one whangs it home dead true. If it doesn't quite go true, don't pulverize it, but tap it out with the narrow end and begin again.

Magic hammer

Remember, we're in no hurry, we're here to enjoy ourselves, so do not accept inaccuracy for the sake of another try. I proceeded exactly the same as I did with the polyester resin, finishing the inside with wax on 0000 grade steel wool.

Every time I changed the position of the ball in the chuck, my little hammer ensured it went true. No trouble turning the box and fitting it either.

Finally I exchanged the chuck arbor for my polishing buff screw and polished the ball impeccably. Then I sent a few of the puzzle

Home-made polishing buff arbor

boxes round the audience for inspection. One member loudly asked, 'Do you supply those magic hammers?' What a good question. I've had that hammer over 40 years and I made it especially for boxwood catheter plugs, tapping them out of the taper chuck when turning the knob end. Twelve bob a gross I got for them until they found some modern replacement at ten times the price – it was only public money.

A colleague who brings me some real teasers of jobs from time to time (and sometimes stays while I do them), observed the magic hammer on many occasions. 'I wish you'd make me one,' he finally asked. He is a fine restorer of things ancient and modern, but not a turner and, to his surprise and delight, one day I did make and present him with one which made my poor old warrior look shabby indeed. This must be five years ago.

Only the other day he affirmed how useful that there hammer has always been. You see, it's just the right shape, it's unable to injure and can be directed more accurately than the next best thing, the handle of a tool.

So there you have the puzzle ball, and the magic hammer. Don't let me find you without them if ever I pop in to see you.

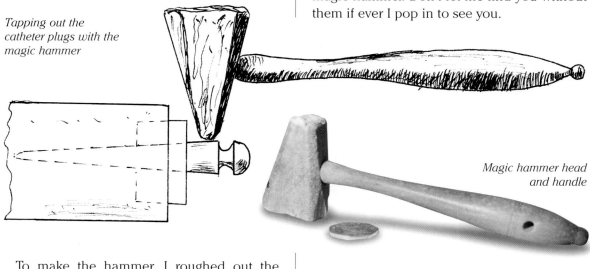

Tapping out the catheter plugs with the magic hammer

Magic hammer head and handle

To make the hammer, I roughed out the head on the circular saw and fixed it in a large Holtzapffel two jaw chuck to drill and cut a course thread, well countersunk. To cut a matching thread on the handle after a simple bit of spindle turning was the work of five minutes in the large, hollow mandrel lathe.

And that hammer, terribly battered, but still quite serviceable, is a constant friend which resides on a nail 2ft (60cm) above my head.

Chapter 20 ● Persevering *with* NEW TOOLS

A favourite old saw I've been known to quote is, 'Blessed is he who expecteth nothing, for he shall not be disappointed.' But, like many twisted clichés which encourage not, I have revised it to suit a more positive outlook, which itself is the result of experience. It now reads, 'Blessed are those who expecteth something

wonderful, for no subsequent disappointment can take away the times of joyful anticipation.' And bad cess to all cynics, say I.

Any good turner may make us self-critical, but just remember, not one of them can do it all. Each one of us has some skill or knowledge that the best of us lack, so the answer is to pursue the positive approach and keep at it.

Above A pair of size 20 screw chasers

Some people – and I believe they're the majority – ignore the 90% success they have and commiserate over the 10% non-success. Note the non-success if you like, but never forget to enjoy your success every day. If you show some people the silver lining, what do they do? Whip out the cloud like trumping an ace. Don't let this apply to you.

I did that with a ⅛in (3.5mm) round nose tool. A friend showed me a high speed steel, Ashley Iles round nose, ⅛ x ⁹⁄₃₂ x 8in (3.5 x 7 x 200mm). Well, I always use a small, triangular saw file, ground to a ⅛in (3.5mm) round nose, but I treated myself to the new one, and furnished it with a beautiful long handle from my sweet willow, *Salix alba*.

Salix alba handle

The yellow catkins of this charm the nostrils with a rare redolence, occasioning congratulation from the odd passer-by in the summer. The pruned branches make unusually handsome, attractive handles, which I polish on the buff.

I like polished tool handles, but not applied polish that flakes. It wasn't always so. Another friend once said he wouldn't pick up my tools in the street and I really think it was that remark that changed my attitude – that and demonstrating of course. I shall never get more than a fraction of my tools in such luxurious handles, but of course, I am a workman, not a dilettante.

FAMILIARITY

I found the new tool so different from my friendly old file (in its even friendlier old handle) that I relegated the proud, shining one to the department of 'Tools to be tried when all

else fails' – if you know what I mean. (For turning bits of old iron and the like.)

Yet today I had the little job of turning narrow recesses in African blackwood and my usual old file didn't want to know. I'm sure tools, like people, have off days (usually because of people). I then tried my Ashley Iles, which hadn't been sharpened since I'd turned mild steel with it, and found it cut like a good'n. And do you know, that one success enhanced my appreciation of the excellent tool.

Prejudice can undermine the best of tools, simply because we aren't used to them. If you could grab a tool and do perfect work, the world would be full of fine craftsmen. We all had to learn by perseverance, so why not recognize that even when you've learnt, new tools still need getting used to.

Here I must again give a plug to the armrest, which must be the easiest tool to reject as awkward and cumbersome, yet, when mastered, becomes such a good friend that its absence would seriously interfere with my normal everyday work. I have occasionally used another long-handled tool (a gouge) as a substitute when an armrest hasn't been available.

MASTERING THE GOUGE

'A nice clean surface straight from the gouge,' says my friend Chris Stott in his superb video, *Turning Boxes*. I'm a second class woodturner myself, and I didn't get certain success trying this cut.

The start is dicey, you need to twist the gouge three-quarters over to the right to begin, and the cut gets underway with the gouge on its side, turning up a bit as it gets to the centre.

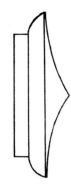

A clean surface cut, straight from the gouge

With the bevel rubbing all the time, the gouge is steered carefully, but confidently, in a hollowing cut. I found it didn't always want to cut, and force doesn't help. Still, I kept trying whenever work called for it.

Then, a job came along for thumb piston heads in boxwood and rosewood. In ivory I make the concave surface with the side of a round nose scraper, but for wood I used a 3⁄8in (10mm) spindle gouge.

As I've always found, it is repetition that teaches you how to succeed – unless the wrong method is used. I did 120 of them using the gouge as described. I learned to manipulate the gouge instead of using force. Quite a slight movement left or right, up or down, will produce the cut you want. The tool soon lets you know when it is happy by cutting well and without stress. You'll know you've conquered the problem when you don't have to think about it. The hands automatically apply the tool correctly when they become accustomed to it.

Writing for *Woodturning* is a two-way benefit for me because, in trying to advise, encourage and interest others I find I'm also learning from others all the time. I've learned that you must allow the tool time to cut. The concave may be going fine, and suddenly the gouge stops cutting for a small pause. If you force it, the surface may be spoiled.

After a second or two, and perhaps a slight corrective movement, the cut will be perfectly finished, but time and care must be taken to end with an unblemished centre by turning off the centre pip without a trace. It takes patience, but it's easy when you know how, and it is these hard-won skills that constitute the joy of woodturning. And I've written all this to prove that years alone don't count for much – in some matters I am the veriest tyro!

EARLY JOBS

I'm going to my shop's log for some reminiscences that may be of interest. Back in 1947, when the 'juice' was connected to my first workshop, almost my first job was half a gross of ebony chest pieces for stethoscopes.

Simple. After cutting the ebony, one end is hubbed to fit the cup chuck with the 2–3in (50–75mm) cutter. The chuck is an iron one stopped with boxwood which is opened to whatever size is needed. These stoppers accumulate and it's seldom necessary to make new ones. After a rub on the ball of whiting (pulverized chalk), the ebony is driven into the chuck – about 1⁄8–5⁄32in (3–4mm) – with a short-handled, 1½lb (680g) ball pein hammer, and the screw is cut to fit the metal counterpart.

Iron cup chuck with boxwood stopper

Any spare piece of material can be used for cutting a matching inside thread, to be fixed in the three jaw, to hold the pieces for turning the other end, and finishing with black French polish. About a day's work at one and tuppence each. I'll wager they're moulded in plastic now.

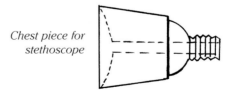

Chest piece for stethoscope

The next orders Bertram sent me were for cigarette tubes, cylinder, trumpet and tulip, for Barrets of Burlington Arcade. The sizes went from 2–7in (50–175mm), with the occasional 10in (250mm).

We did a variety of work for Barrets; teething rings, rattles, swizzle sticks, screwed and plain toothpicks, shoehorns, collar studs, peppermills, condiment sets, dice, necklaces, brooches and 'whistles for calling them in from the garden,' as ancient Mr Henty, the dear little man who kept the shop, used quaintly to say.

The rattles were rather nice, made from old billiard balls. We could buy them from Friedlein, in the Minories, London. He kept a barrel of them at a shilling each. The balls were 2in (50mm) or so, and the rattle was 1⅜–1⅝in (36–40mm). You'd get about eight good ones out of a dozen. The other four would be too cracked, but still might be useful.

We made them with a teething ring at one end and a whistle at t'other, and a brass bell inside. They cost Barrets 12 shillings each, and sold at a very high figure. I was rather surprised, but Bertram said, 'Barrets are paying eighty quid a week for that little shop.' He never minded what his customers charged for work he'd made – that was their business.

I struggled along with bits and pieces Bertram sent my way. He was turning and carving away in his little shop at Badsey, near Evesham, in the beautiful Cotswolds, so we didn't meet very often. By off-loading the general run-o'-the-mill work, he was now free to tackle projects he had long admired, but seldom had time for, except in the form of repairs.

BERTRAM'S CHESS SETS

It is frustrating to be faking up dead work, and have no opportunity to make original things. So now I was taking the strain, as it were, Bertram took advantage of this by making ornate chess sets. Now, although he copied old sets, he always adapted them to a greater or lesser extent and there was a wide variety, both in design and in quality of workmanship: some were superb and some were not.

Bertram came from a trade where speed governed all, and if someone could do your work a ha'penny cheaper, you lost that particular job. The chess trade can be extremely miserly. Some want the very best and to pay the very least. Bertram's London buyer wanted some of the best ornate collectors' sets, which he was pleased to make. At the same time, he also wanted all the regular Staunton sets, which of course held Bertram up. It would have solved the problem if I made the Stauntons, but as my overheads were much higher, the man kept poor old Bertram slogging away rather than pay another £2 on a 4½in (115mm) set.

> ## HIS OVERHEADS were negligible, his wants were few, and such a man who enjoys his work is the wealthiest of all

So Bertram used to cut ivory for three sets of 4½in (115mm) Stauntons, put 'em in a bucket of water to soak, and slash 'em off in a week. He used just one day to carve the 12 knights. They were undeniably crude, but as the old man said, 'someone will like them.' The £36 he got for the three sets in best African ivory didn't allow time for perfection. When the famous firm of Jaques made Staunton chess, they had a team of turners and carvers. The turners didn't carve and the carvers didn't turn, so, in effect, they were a mass-produced assembly line job. Yet customers expected Bertram to make the whole set – which, as a one-man set production, was a work of art – for the same price, or even cheaper than the mass-produced job. They were still lovely Jones' sets though, and he had no complaints.

When he began a fine set however, he took his time and turned out a number of lovely sets. Whenever they surface and come on the market, as they do occasionally, they reach the £1,000 mark, and Bertram is down in the catalogues as a notable chess maker.

He might be said to have been shamefully taken advantage of, yet I do not think he would have minded. His overheads were negligible, his wants were few, and such a man who enjoys his work is the wealthiest of all. If he gets a pension as well and does a bit of fishing when he chooses, he's a king.

DRILLING TIPS

Mastering the job of drilling cigarette tubes wasn't easy, and they were to make up a large part of my trade for years to come. Smoking was respectable then, but now cigarette tubes are more or less obsolete.

The old hollow mandrel lathe I was using at the time was hardly rock steady, as it should be for such work, and I had to experiment a lot to get my spear drills to cut nicely.

They had to be softened by heating to a cherry red, hammered flat at the end, ground to shape with nice cutting edges, then hardened by heating again to cherry red, and tempered by quenching for an inch in light oil, rubbing abrasive paper over that inch (quickly) so that the colours could be seen running up from the hot steel.

wrote a step-by-step procedure for drilling in a 'tips and wheezers' book. It went like this:

1 A well oiled lathe vibrates less.
2 Tools must always be sharp and drills perfectly straight and oiled. (I keep an oil pot for this.)
3 Centre the tube in the three jaw, with pencil mark if necessary, and tighten securely.
4 Make a perfect countersink with the square tool.
5 Carefully make a small hole with a pilot drill centred on the armrest.
6 With the armrest close to the work, true the hole with second drill.
7 Carry on drilling – clearing and oiling carefully as you go, and if you still find the drill has deviated, mark the top of the tube with pencil, which will indicate that extra care will be needed when meeting it from the other end.
8 The most important thing, as in all good work, is to let the tools cut without force. If you need force, sharpen the damn things. (That's how I wrote it.)

The smallest deviation at the start will increase as the drill advances, possibly breaking through the side. Sometimes the drill

Spear drill

When a light straw colour reached the point, the whole was finally quenched and the drill was sharpened on a medium India stone. Quenching in water can make metal brittle and possibly break in the tube.

I made several sizes from 13in (330mm) rods of silver steel. Your chance of getting a true meeting when you drill from the other end, using a slightly larger drill, depends on the dead accurate start of the hole. The armrest, of course, ensures a true start with a pilot drill. I

will twist into a corkscrew if soft, or break if too hard. Then back to the forge – my old gas fire.

In those early days I'd never heard of D-bits, which I found when I met the Society of Ornamental Turners. These useful drills come in sizes up to about 1½in (38mm), and the small ones for the tobacco trade were known as pipe bits.

This drill is ³⁄₃₂in (2mm), silver steel, ground or filed exactly down to the diametral line for about ¼in (6mm), and the end stoned to a

Square tool and small D-bit

slight angle. A little experimentation is necessary, and you'll soon know when you've got it right.

A well-oiled, sharp D-bit, given an accurate start, will be twice as likely to maintain a true hole, without wandering, than a spear drill.

The bigger D-bits are excellent for boring true holes, and are usually used in ascending sizes until the required diameter is reached. They work rather like reamers, and I often begin with fast cutting spear drills and open accurately with a D-bit. They are splendid for

making flat-bottomed holes when screwing chessmen and small components. Even Bertram, when I introduced them to him, found them useful. They aren't usually made today, and the only ones I have ever seen have all been made by Holtzapffel.

The D-bits can be advanced by the tailstock, the handle having a reinforced countersink at the end, and a transverse hole for a tommy bar. I have some that are 1ft (305mm) long.

I'll finish here with a quote from my prized box of Bertram's letters – full of useful anecdotes, advice and tips. November 28, 1948: 'Don't give the Government money – they only waste it. I've just had my income tax demand. I've got to pay 15 shillings in two instalments. I suppose they are going to build a couple of dreadnoughts.'

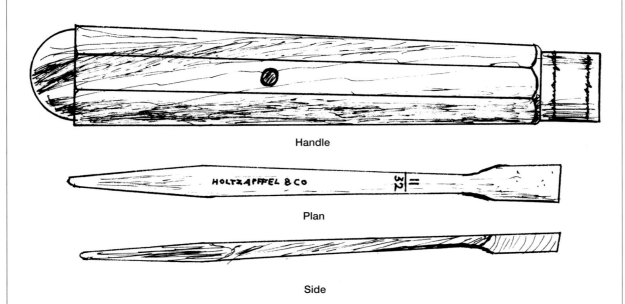

Handle

Plan

Side

A D-bit blade and handle with transverse hole

Health
and SAFETY

I t is only too true that familiarity breeds contempt, and where machinery is concerned, there can be some hard lessons learned. Unfortunately, many 'old sweats' of the workshop who should know better – and that includes me I'm afraid – set poor examples in the matter of safety. In fairness, however, it must be said that one soon becomes aware of the dangers, and although a professional often does things he wouldn't advise a beginner to do, he knows very well how far he can safely go. So here are just a few workshop necessities, whether you are a novice or an old hand.

Always wear eye protection. Ordinary specs suit me – I started with plain glass – but I wear goggles as an extra when grinding. There are some sophisticated remedies that nullify the effects of dust, and it's worth having the best if the atmosphere is at all dangerous. The atmosphere in my workshop isn't dangerous (or very seldom), so a cheap dust mask is excellent. I'm amazed at what I used to (unthinkingly) endure though!

Floppy sleeves, ties, and loose, long hair are to be avoided, as are sandals and bare feet. Stout leather footwear will prevent injury from falling tools or anything else flying about a workshop. Wandering leads should be out of the way or they'll lie in wait to trip the unwary.

A couple of luxuries I would have for myself if it wasn't far too late! One is to keep all tools and equipment neatly and securely stored. This is a praiseworthy aim which is easy if one's work is not too varied, and a change of venue occurs once every ten years or so. But try telling an old blacksmith (whose forge, over many years has accumulated so much impedimenta, filling every space and hanging on every beam) that he should keep his equipment neatly and securely stored! Sufficient – and miraculous – that he nearly always knows where to lay hands on what he wants. His principal tools are always kept in accustomed places. Second luxury is to keep tools sharp and oiled if necessary. I have a regular grinding session, but with plenty of tools, I don't usually have to stop for one unless it's the only one of its kind. It is always a mistake to carry on working with a blunt tool, which I have done, to my cost!

Haste is a turner's enemy. Always check the set-up before starting the lathe – it's too late when the chuck key flies up and catches you, or something that should've been tightened or removed wasn't.

I am a jaw chuck man, but the three and four jaw scroll chucks are quite unsuitable for safe use until the leading edges and corners of the jaws have been rounded on the grinder thoroughly – this will save many lacerations. When the jaws are gripping small work, the jaw slots are exposed and when sanding, the sharp edges can severely nick one's hand. I always file these sharp edges off the slots, which are not hardened. Surprisingly, I find I have to be extra careful when using other people's lathes, as some of them are dangerously unground. I've thought of getting shares in Elastoplast!

A First Aid box should always be handy because, where machines and sharp tools are, danger is not far away, however remote in normal circumstances.

I know at first hand the danger of fire! Where shavings are, open fires should not be, and even worn leads can cause unexpected conflagration – and when a fire starts or takes hold with frightening rapidity, it is too late to read the instructions on your fire extinguisher! This happened to me, and I couldn't get the extinguisher to work. The fire blanket, an old sack, failed! I was saved by an armful of wet grass cuttings I had – amazingly – outside the shop door.

I have lived my life amid open belts and shafting, and often been quite careless with it, but my lathes are all foot-controlled, and I often stop and run the belt back by hand when unscrewing. I have never felt any danger from belts and pulleys, which are really in very safe positions. Closed in, fixed speed lathes are far more dangerous and unfriendly to this old turner, but we seem to be stuck with them, and today pulleys must be heard and not seen! I never advise anyone how to go about turning, which is an entirely personal thing, so I take no responsibility. If turners feel safer and happier making covers to guard belts and pulleys I commend them for doing so. I explain everything I do with full coverage of safety angles and I know that my methods with my light and fully controlled tackle are usually safer than some heavy duty, closed-in monsters that may pass the factory inspector, but would frighten me! Actually, I feel safer in the turning shop than in the house!

137

Metric
Conversion TABLE

Inches to millimetres and centimetres

mm – millimetres   cm – centimetres

inches	mm	cm	inches	cm	inches	cm
⅛	3	0.3	9	22.9	30	76.2
¼	6	0.6	10	25.4	31	78.7
⅜	10	1.0	11	27.9	32	81.3
½	13	1.3	12	30.5	33	83.8
⅝	16	1.6	13	33.0	34	86.4
¾	19	1.9	14	35.6	35	88.9
⅞	22	2.2	15	38.1	36	91.4
1	25	2.5	16	40.6	37	94.0
1¼	32	3.2	17	43.2	38	96.5
1½	38	3.8	18	45.7	39	99.1
1¾	44	4.4	19	48.3	40	101.6
2	51	5.1	20	50.8	41	104.1
2½	64	6.4	21	53.3	42	106.7
3	76	7.6	22	55.9	43	109.2
3½	89	8.9	23	58.4	44	111.8
4	102	10.2	24	61.0	45	114.3
4½	114	11.4	25	63.5	46	116.8
5	127	12.7	26	66.0	47	119.4
6	152	15.2	27	68.6	48	121.9
7	178	17.8	28	71.1	49	124.5
8	203	20.3	29	73.7	50	127.0

About *the* AUTHOR

Bill Jones is the last of a five-generation family of hardwood and ivory turners. His grandfather, Lewis Jones, 1850–1914, lived by his skill as a turner and carver and could remember his father and grandfather being in the trade. Bill's father Bertram, 1885–1969, was a noted turner and carver, principally of chessmen. Two of Bertram's brothers were bone, ivory and horn turners, and Bill's brother and sister could turn well before they went on to other things.

Bill has been a turner from the age of 14, apart from five wartime years as an engine fitter in the RAF, starting his own business in 1947. The trade had begun rapidly decreasing then, and today, Bill is one of the last of the old 'bone grubbers', as hardwood and ivory turners used to be called.

Meeting the Society of Ornamental Turners in 1948, just after they began, provided a tremendous stimulus for Bill's turning aspirations: the incredible work of some of the masters of the art, who were still working at that time, encouraged him to learn, teach, and above all write about his experiences.

For good turners who can build a reputation, says Bill, the trade will never be finished. Bill contributes regular articles to *Woodturning* magazine, sharing his obvious enjoyment and his lifetime's experience in turning; this book contains the first 20 of these.

Index

TITLES available *from* GMC Publications

Carving Birds and Beasts GMC Publications

Practical Tips for Turners and Carvers GMC Publications

Practical Tips for Woodturners GMC Publications

Spindle Turning GMC Publications

Useful Woodturning Projects GMC Publications

Woodturning Techniques GMC Publications

Woodworkers' Career and Educational Source Book
   GMC Publications

Woodworking Plans and Projects GMC Publications

40 More Woodworking Plans and Projects GMC Publications

Green Woodwork Mike Abbott

Easy to Make Dolls' House Accessories Andrea Barham

Making Period Dolls' House Accessories Andrea Barham

Making Little Boxes from Wood John Bennett

Woodturning Masterclass Tony Boase

Furniture Restoration and Repair for Beginners
   Kevin Jan Bonner

Furniture Restoration Kevin Jan Bonner

Woodturning Jewellery Hilary Bowen

Decorative Woodturning Techniques Hilary Bowen

The Incredible Router Jeremy Broun

Electric Woodwork Jeremy Broun

Woodcarving: A Complete Course Ron Butterfield

Making Fine Furniture: Projects Tom Darby

Restoring Rocking Horses Clive Green & Anthony Dew

Make Your Own Dolls' House Furniture Maurice Harper

Embroidery Tips and Hints Harold Hayes

Seat Weaving Ricky Holdstock

Multi-Centre Woodturning Ray Hopper

Complete Woodfinishing Ian Hosker

Woodfinishing Handbook Ian Hosker

Woodturning: A Source Book of Shapes John Hunnex

Illustrated Woodturning Techniques John Hunnex

Making Shaker Furniture Barry Jackson

Upholstery: A Complete Course David James

Upholstery Techniques and Projects David James

The Upholsterer's Pocket Reference Book David James

Designing and Making Wooden Toys Terry Kelly

Making Dolls' House Furniture Patricia King

Making Victorian Dolls' House Furniture Patricia King

Making and Modifying Woodworking Tools Jim Kingshott

The Workshop Jim Kingshott

Sharpening: The Complete Guide Jim Kingshott

Sharpening Pocket Reference Book Jim Kingshott

Turning Wooden Toys Terry Lawrence

Making Board, Peg and Dice Games Jeff & Jennie Loader

Making Wooden Toys and Games Jeff & Jennie Loader

Bert Marsh: Woodturner Bert Marsh

The Complete Dolls' House Book Jean Nisbett

The Secrets of the Dolls' House Makers Jean Nisbett

Wildfowl Carving, Volume 1 Jim Pearce

Wildfowl Carving, Volume 2 Jim Pearce

Architecture for Dolls' Houses Joyce Percival

Make Money from Woodturning Ann & Bob Phillips

The Complete Pyrography Stephen Poole

Woodcarving Tools, Materials and Equipment Chris Pye

Carving on Turning Chris Pye

Tatting Collage: Adventurous Ideas for Tatters Lindsay Rogers

Cross Stitch on Colour Sheena Rogers

Making Tudor Dolls' Houses Derek Rowbottom

Making Georgian Dolls' Houses Derek Rowbottom

Making Period Dolls' House Furniture
   Derek & Sheila Rowbottom

Woodturning: A Foundation Course Keith Rowley

Keith Rowley's Woodturning Projects Keith Rowley

Turning Miniatures in Wood John Sainsbury

Colouring Techniques for Woodturners Jan Saunders

Pleasure and Profit from Woodturning Reg Sherwin

Making Unusual Miniatures Graham Spalding

Woodturning Wizardry David Springett

Adventures in Woodturning David Springett

Carving Realistic Birds David Tippey

Furniture Projects Rod Wales

Decorative Woodcarving Jeremy Williams